Fermi Paradox

Where Are All the Aliens?

(History of the Famous Debate Over the Existence of Aliens)

David Carter

Published By **Phil Dawson**

David Carter

Fermi Paradox: Where Are All the Aliens? (History of the Famous Debate Over the Existence of Aliens)

ISBN 978-1-77485-892-9

Legal & Disclaimer

The information contained in this ebook is not designed to replace or take the place of any form of medicine or professional medical advice. The information in this ebook has been provided for educational & entertainment purposes only.

The information contained in this book has been compiled from sources deemed reliable, and it is accurate to the best of the Author's knowledge; however, the Author cannot guarantee its accuracy and validity and cannot be held liable for any errors or omissions. Changes are periodically made to this book. You must consult your doctor or get professional medical advice before using any of the suggested remedies, techniques, or information in this book.

Table Of Contents

Introduction

Fermi

"The dimensions and nature of the universe leads our belief that a number of technologically advanced civilizations exist. But, this notion seems unlogical and contradicts our lack of evidence from observation to prove it. It could be that (1) the assumption that was made initially is false and that intelligent, technologically advanced life is far more scarce than we imagine, or (2) our observations are insufficient and we haven't discovered these yet, or (3) our search methods are flawed and we're not seeking the proper indicators and (4) Intelligent life is designed to degrade itself." The Fermi Paradox

The issue of man's place in the universe has been debated in every culture from the very beginning of recorded the history of. In the absence of evidence to support otherwise, debates about the possibility of a different Earth from its solitary existence have been largely conceptual. The current debate is motivated by the emergence of mysterious phenomena throughout the ages in the space and outer space in such a way that contact with alien civilizations is depicted in the oldest depictions of art.

In the drawings on rocks of Valcamonica in the Italian Lombardy Plain, tantalizing etchings indicate that the ancient people had the same kind of visual appearances as the ones that were present to modern-day man. These drawings that date to the year 10,000 BC serve as a counterpart to today's claimed evidence of contact. Apart from aerial crafts images, they also depict light-emitting helmeted human figures containing unidentified artifacts. These kinds of images can be seen not just in the earth's vast landmass however, they can also be found in ancient tablets, temples, and massive western cathedrals.

Within both Old and the New Testaments in the Bible the appearance of what appears to be supernatural creatures is typically typified by Ezekiel's visions about the "wheel," interpreted by many as the appearance of a "heavenly" object or creature that is from The Seraphic realm.

Similar visions are also associated with angelic appearances at the time of Christ's birth Christ and continue up to Book of Revelation at the New Testament's close. Without a scientific language to evaluate these events The angelic metaphor in the "heavenly hierarchy" model was the preferred name for a non-scientific populace. The depictions are revered and regarded as the true truth of the time by millions of people around the globe. If they represent real-life events and creatures that are real, such as such as the angel in the garden of Eden's flaming sword the annunciation of Mary along with the appearances of the heralds before the shepherds could be seen as any of a variety of phenomena using a scientific view.

As technology advancements and the development of flying planes became a reality UFO sightings became more frequent, as did the fascination with possible contact with aliens. As incidents such as those at Roswell resulted in conspiracy theories and a surge of interest of those who claimed that the government was concealing evidence of aliens' existence, governments all over the world were secretly studying UFO sightings in the 20th century.

In all the above, it's not innovative for scientists in the early 20th century hold an informal lunchtime conversation where the hunt for alien life is discussed and the question about where it might be isn't too difficult to answer. However, a stir was created in a way that was not entirely innocent by the physicist Enrico Fermi voiced his "casual lunchtime remark"[1 while in front of his colleagues in 1950. The distinguished group of colleagues comprised Edward Teller, a Hungarian physicist Herbert York, am American nuclear physicist, whose family tree included Mohawk origins and Emil Konopinski, a nuclear scientist of Polish origin. Fermi himself was an Italian-American who was born in Rome was well-known for his work in developing a statistical foundation for subatomic phenomena, his work on the alterations to nuclear structure caused by neutrons, as well as for establishing the first chain reaction controlled caused by nuclear fission. To manage the atom, Fermi created his first reactor for nuclear energy. A brilliant mathematician, he developed the field of statistical mechanics and was awarded the Nobel Prize over a decade before asking his pivotal question. The four men made up an important portion of the research core in the Manhattan Project that developed and developed the first atomic bomb.

Despite the complex discussion that is believed to be following, Fermi's frequently-asked question quickly became a hot topic within the scientific community and was referred to as"the Fermi Paradox. The subsequent discussions on our quest for extraterrestrials have grown to the point that numerous lists of answers to the question are appearing every year. Not only is the underlying of the problem surrounded by theories of speculation however, the validity of the term"paradox" is in itself questioned. Merriam-Webster defines a paradox as "a statement that seems contrary to common sense, but may be true."[2The definition is akin to this contradictory assertion with the caveat that it may appear to be true in the beginning. In every story of the Fermi exchange the physicist asked an inquiry into what extraterrestrial life may be hiding, but not an assertion that it was even present. A statement that contradicts itself to be valid on an initial hearing, it must be an inverse decision in the case of extraterrestrial research, since it is a prerequisite for a first evidence. It has to start as an untrue assertion or be thought to be. The evidence-based science has to proceed in a manner that is skeptical, moving by moving from the most skeptical point towards a possible reverse. In the same way, the Merriam-Webster paradox demands a premise grounded in a rational model. Without any external observations and our own being the only that is available. Human technological, physiological and cultural structure could be a fragile foundation that we can rely on in the face of several possible galactic universes. But, during the initial research, scientists had no other choice than to put it at the heart of the research's reasoning.

What is thought to be"the "paradox" was formulated in the years following the time when the discussion "petered out,"[3 as per Teller. While he was claiming that we've yet to meet neighbours in our universe Earth has not, and yet hasn't experienced a single incident of visible contact. Simply put the reason for this is there is a hugeness of the possible residences of aliens determined with care based on our current understanding hasn't been able to provide any evidence of intelligent alien life.

Chapter 1: Introduction To The Origins Of The Paradox

The issue of whether or not humans are the only race in the universe is still an ongoing issue in the field of human research. In the past when there was no way to resolve the issue in either direction The issue has since been largely discarded in its rhetorical nature. As we move into the early phase of space travel develop technology to improve electromagnetic and visible signals, and make the existence of aliens a common course of inquiry, Earth is no longer satisfied to simply look at the stars and imagine. The realms of philosophy, religion and science fiction are able to play with the topic of the existence of life off the planet. It is now the perfect time for science to attempt its hand at this issue.

Faithful believers cite numerous alien appearances throughout the two Testaments from the Bible. The religion has approached the issue by relying on faith that is untested, removing this inquiry of the Scientific Method. Science isn't qualified to affirm that the people of the Scriptures did not have any evidence in their experiences if they are accepted as real-life possibilities. Without the benefits of research and analysis in language, early religions described their experiences the only method they were able to. The symbolic pictures of angels, the pillars of flame as well as "Elijah's Wheel" could be given distinct dialectic interpretations when evidence-based research is gaining momentum.

When it comes to science fiction, scientists must acknowledge that the works aimed to stimulate the human capacity for fantasies have "created an expression on the human imagination."[4The human element is not a thing that can be brushed off , as a variety of real-world reality have emerged out of the industry that produces entertainment. Inspiration and imagination are the same human qualities which led to space exploration in beginning, and a lot of Hollywood sources are based on research conducted by actual scientists.

The philosopher also affixes his thoughts from his most influential historical figures to theories of logic that might appear unimportant to some at the microscopically level. However, philosophical ideas can sometimes be successful in the larger context of physical and human logic. As with the worshiper philosopher, the philosopher is unable to identify the truths behind one's experiences. The same is true for a philosopher. an physicist with a theoretical perspective thinking out of his time will not provide a significant advance to his time.

A systematic search for intelligent life in the Earth's close stars was developed during the initial space race in the Soviet Union, and through the first human-manned space missions. The program was a bit off the beaten path of U.S. agenda for space exploration, the scientists who were involved in the hunt for aliens were not sure of the success of the program. They were stung by the stigma of being a fringe activity without a clear endpoint that could put a whole career in uncertainty. But, the idea of alien contact was in the state of alert after a series of flying objects that were not identified and a number of investigative panels in the past. The majority were initiated through the militaries. The astronomers of the past have conducted studies of what was once thought as being exoplanets or "artifacts" when seen from the distance. One of the most notable examples is Percival Lowell, an American scientist, businessman, and astronomer, declared his belief that the channels of Mars were constructed artificially by a mysterious civilization. In many instances the thing that was seen from a distance turned in reality to have been the result of optical distortion.

The sequence of important factors that led to Fermi Paradox. Fermi Paradox came from a Manhattan Project panel discussion about the flying saucer and superluminal traveling however, the subject Fermi and his colleagues were discussing had a history of scientific theories and principles to base their work on. They started with a solid theory that suggests that in our galaxy, called the Milky Way, a large number of stars are present that are at least as similar with the Sun. This leads to the speculation of a theoretical possibility that there is among these stars an adequate number of Earth-like planets. Out of the 100 billion stars that are known, the majority of them are red dwarfs. However, there is a small fraction of 17% look like the Sun. Scientists working on a investigation of the University of British Columbia estimate that around 6 billion stars have Earth-like planets in orbit. The data for this study is provided mostly by NASA's Kepler mission that discovered exoplanets using what was the most advanced technology of the day. Another study conducted by University of Nottingham. University of Nottingham suggests that there are 36 intelligent species within the galaxy. According to the UBC study, which is confined to a strictly defined requirement of habitable planets that are rocky Earth-sized, with existing water - warns us that there is nothing found. The study instead "placed an upper limit for the number of Earth-like planets that may be in the vicinity of sun-like stars."[55.

In line with the human model, the limitations in mass and size of the bodies could be met by the distance and rotational behaviour when they are circling their stars. Scientists believe that generally the planets that have sufficient likeness to Earth are much older. Based on our own records of human evolution, which is a short time period, when compared to the entire history of Earth there are a few moons may have evolved advanced types living things. If they exist, the natural desire to expand and expand could have led to the possibility to travel interstellarly.

A lot of Earth-bound scientists are aligned against the idea of interstellar space travel, and those who aren't agree with them acknowledge that the challenges to achieve it are overwhelming. If it happens at all currently, we will not be witnessing the event, nor will they be able to witness it in the years to follow in 2021. Paul Sutter, astrophysicist at Ohio State University, makes the argument that interstellar space transport is "technically possible,"[6 and that no law of physics prohibit it. Sutter adds that the process of overcoming the inherent difficulties of achieving this goal can be "a real problem in the neck."[77.

NASA's Voyager probes which are escape missions that are not designed to return to earth, are "going nowhere very fast,"[8Sutter says. Sutter However, they will be able to reach Proxima Centauri in approximately 80,000 years. To be manned spacecraft acceptable the vessel has to begin at 1/10th rate of light. The speed required is a lot of energy and if the fuel is carried aboard it will impede the advantages. The latest Breakthrough Starshot Project suggests an Earth-bound laser directed towards ships equipped with a solar sail reflective. The project plans on creating a fleet of vessels that can travel to Alpha Centauri in fewer than four years. The sail will provide external power, which would eliminate the issue of thrust versus weight. But at 100 Gigawatts which is equivalent to the power output of all nuclear reactors around the globe The craft will be required to weigh the same as an ordinary paperclip, and for the next four decades, the craft will be exposed to every destructive force that exists in space.

If an alien civilization is able to be able to overcome these challenges and join the human need for expansion, achieving the entire width and length of the Milky Way should be possible. It would be accomplished through either personal travel, probes, or various forms of artificial intelligence, reintroducing variants of the weight- versus-propulsion-and-mass dilemma. If it is successful, scientists have set the timeline for the galactic dominance to be only of 10 million years. The fact the planet's age is older than the rest of the planet is a source of frustration for some scientists as to why we haven't been visited by aliens, which is Fermi's initial complaint. The fact that no human encounter is confirmed as a fact and there is no discernible signal that could signal alien presence, bolsters Fermi's observations to form an untruth.

The practices of other civilizations has to be an expression of the human desire for expansion and establishing control over newly conquered territories and civilizations. The participants at the initial discussion confirmed that a civilization that has the bare minimum of rocket technology might eventually be able to cover the galactic distance one end to the next. In addition, with sufficient "imperial incentive"[9to travel to every corner of the galaxy, these travellers might be able to cover the entire distance in a mere 10-million years. The short timeframe would be able to place each star and system within "the wings of the empire."[10When compared to the length of time that the galaxy has been in this time frame could prove to be an "quick exercise."[11In the event that the barriers to interstellar travel eliminated at least conceptually, the logic of the alien's inability to show up is considered in a variety of scenarios, primarily as confirmation the existence of aliens. It is believed that the civilization at issue is in the process of exploring but hasn't reached our area at this point. One speculated that "We live in the woods which is far from the metropolis of galactic center."[12Perhaps colonization or travel is feasible, however, for a reason or other the alien race has decided not to undertake the trip, perhaps in order to not interfere with an already established human civilization. The possibility is definitely there. Earth has been able to create a steady and distinct signal that reaches further into space every day. The power of the media signals has been that concentrated since the time of the early days of television and radio that hiding will no longer be an option.

Fermi was killed in 1954 however the optimistic vision of his final paradox, which was rife of excuses about aliens' inability to show up on time, began to take on an entirely new life. The optimistic nature of the hunt for intelligent aliens was a popular theme in the years following his death supported by the companion theories. One of these is the case one of Frank Drake, American astrophysicist and long-time director of SETI. in 1961 Drake moved Fermi's restaurant to the conference room for the SETI event located in Green Bank, West Virginia. In his latest theory of extraterrestrials commonly referred to as"the Drake Equation or Green Bank Equation He claimed to estimate the number of advanced civilizations that exist within the galaxy. Alongside the institutionalized investigation of extraterrestrials various areas of research played a role in the debate. The conference's profile was in sharp contrast to the scientists who were working on the first atomic weapon, with the goal of controlling the outcome of an nuclear collision.

A photo taken by Drake in 2017

In Drake's form, N represented the approximate amount of technological civilizations within the Milky Way. It was calculated by calculating R, which is the rate of formation of stars within this parameter. The percentage of stars with planet systems was represented as the fp symbol, while ne represented the amount of systems that a human would consider to be ecologically appropriate to live in. The proportion of planets which life might develop was designated fl, and fi was the amount of intelligent life could evolve. Civilizations that had advanced enough to have radio communications were called fc. L determined the average time of life of a specific civilization. In a way, the speed of destruction by civilizations identified them as "advanced." Drake figured that if a tiny fraction of advanced civilizations escaped the threat of both exterior and self-destruction, then our closest neighbors should be no more than 100 lights years from us.

The Drake Equation brought along not only the inevitable speculations that plagued Fermi and his coworkers, but their optimism too. The belief that we are the only ones within the Universe has been the semblance of arrogance, and the denial of mathematical probabilities. However each step of Drake's progress added a degree of uncertainty equal to the one in the beginning discussion. One skeptical scientist in the scientific community pointed out that no flying machine has flown in faith, therefore with no proof, the score is in a tie at zero.

Chapter 2: Refusal The Paradox

The only point that is available to skeptical people, the absence of any evidence of intelligent alien life up to date, is the sole importance in Hart's arguments. To prevail, it must be able to eliminate all kinds of exaggerated circumstance and inter-cultural differences that could hinder the appearance of extraterrestrials.

Hart was not taken lightly after completing his mathematics undergraduate course at Cornell and the Ph.D. in Astronomy at Princeton. Since the central argument was the lack of any indication of extraterrestrial involvement, he named this truth "Fact A."[13Based on this assumption, Hart set Drake's calculation of the existence of extraterrestrials at zero. Jason Wright of Penn State University reviewed Hart's beliefs and, instead of voting against them, Wright came up with a different approach to enhancing the extraterrestrial intelligence search. The theory is that after the alien's energy store is exhausted, it will be recognized by the infrared spectrum as "waste of heat." This could lead to an unorthodox conclusion. If Hart proves to be correct or at the very most appear to be so the focus should shift to the biggest civilizations that are putting the most energy into. In the same way If Hart is not correct, then searching for smaller societies in the Milky Way is likely to yield more results. Wright's conclusion from re-reading Hart was that the continuing exploration is worthy of the time and effort. Drake's optimism and Hart's pessimism gave an inch of conclusiveness to a solution, or a dispelling of the paradox. Instead, they only marked the patience levels of every scientist. The argument that the bus does not exist simply because it hasn't come to its destination is becoming increasingly obsolete. The anti-extraterrestrial view still carries a whiff of planetary elitism and denial of reasonable math to many in a day where even "Fact A" is under suspicion. In the meantime, technology is growing as the number of exoplanets discovered explodes and new avenues for exploration are being added to the ones already that are already in place. Wright states that an expanded discussion is being held on the "oft-forgotten"[14five dimensions and their relation to the three dimensions of time, space and gravity.

Frank Tipler, Professor of Physics at Tulane University, supported Hart's argument in a research paper that was published in The Royal Astronomical Quarterly Journal in 1980. In a paper that was categorically titled Extraterrestrial Intelligent Beings Don't Exist Tipler dismissed the biological entity from discussion in line with a renowned group of biologists , which included Theodosius D. Dobzhansky George Gaylord Simpson, J. Francois, Francisco Ayala as well as Ernst Mayr. The idea that interstellar travel could ensure the exploration of the galaxy and its colonization within a short period of timespan, he argued for one "self-reproducing universal constructor."[15This is capable of making any kind of device, based on Von Neumann's theory that machines with advanced technology in computing is possible. The theory has been called"Tipler's "replicating probe argument"[16 as well as the "self-replicating spacecraft"[17 theory. Although it sounds like a reaffirmation of the multi-civilization universe , after all Tipler chooses the human being as the sole candidate capable of creating an automated unit.

Tipler's view of life was different from that of the most renowned scientists working in astronomy and related areas. Tipler was awarded the distinction of a Ph.D. in Global General Relativity which was developed in the work of Hawking along with Penrose. He also was an authority on Quantum Field Theory and various computing fields. A stark contrast to his colleagues However, he believed the fundamentals of these fields proved God's existence. God. Because the Biblical civilizations were not able to provide an appropriate scientific language to describe the phenomenon they claimed to be witnessing, Tipler offered to provide the necessary language. One of his most fervent claims is "as as long as you're utilizing quantum mechanics and general relativity and quantum mechanics, you must believe that God exists."[18In a sign of being eager to put his beliefs against the evidence, Tipler openly stated the following "if you (atheists) would like to wage war, I will be victorious in it."[1919

The question of whether or not Tipler wanted to break the laws of physics in order to perform actions described as "miraculous" is subject to scrutiny by scientists like himself. But his innovative and compelling scientific argument for the universe of a god could be a proof of the human being as a marvellous and unrivaled work. This is in line with the belief of certain religions which see our universe to be a huge collection of rooms through which Earthlings could eventually be able to enter in a similar fashion to Jesus's reference to the various rooms in God's house.

The people who are not entirely convinced of the unique and exclusive Earth civilization argue their case through the ongoing discovery of planets that resemble Earth on which similar evolutions might take place. The level of resemblance to Earth conditions is dependent on the extremes scientists are willing to consider. As we discover more about extremeophiles in our planet and witness the creative adaptations to the forces that normally be fatal to their inhabitants and their scales are altered.

Fermi asked the question many years prior to the finding of alien planets however, he could have imagined their existence. The previously unobserved bodies are fueling curiosity in the potential cosmic horizon. It's "vast and old,"[20approximately around 92 billion light-years in diameter and expanding as the bodies separate. The estimated time span of the Milky Way is set at 13.2 billion years, a period of time that has left neighbouring civilizations with plenty of time in which to spread and investigate. Since Fermi's discovery 3000 newly discovered planets were found, some in unimaginable distances and scientists have surpassed the idea that a new life form is found on the earth. There is life within the compositional chemical makeup of atmospheric atmospheres and even in water bodies with compositions that are different from our current one. From the recently discovered Sun-like stars one out of five has an sphere that is similar to Earth enough to be worth looking into. No matter how we modify or extend our definition of habitability the standard human model tends to include a flexible Circumstellar

Habitable Zone dependent in the user-generated model. The inner edge of the ring in this zone is the limit at which the orb can circumnavigate the star and not lose its oceans. The outer edge also is the longest distance that a planet can travel from its star before settling. The concept was first introduced during the year prior to Fermi's demise in the year before Fermi's death by Hubertus Strughold, in his work, The Green and Red Planet The Physiological Study of the possibility of Life on Mars. As time has passed, our adherence towards the carbon-based model has been loosened to include elements of the base such like methane and ammonia.

Accordingly, while proponents of"human "specialism" have used the lack of evidence as the only reason to disprove being aliens, and those who believe in aliens have relied on astronomical odds and the infancy the hunt this paradox is now taking on more extensive existence than the original Fermi inquiry. SETI, NASA, assorted scientific experts as well as a large number of people "entrenched in the thought process of alien civilizations"[21are launching the rebuttal of the Hart-Tipler-based stance. The most frequently used argument in opposition to this "vacant space" theory is to argue that aliens didn't appear because of the physical challenges associated with their appearance. There are a myriad of reasons the reason why they choose not to appear at all and another suggests that they might have already visited and were not within our narrow band of time on our planet. If they were too young to have a human-like shape, their presence could be lost with the dinosaurs. There is a strong argument for the possibility that they've developed too slowly for them to make it to the next stage currently and would require more centuries to advance in technology. They would be in the same position as Earth. The Hart-Tipler argument remains a nonsensical one. While, SETI and its devotees observe the Kepler Telescope expanding the catalogue of exoplanets, as well as making use of growing computing power for optical and radio wave search.

The Kepler Telescope was able to spend 9 years orbiting the universe, serving as the first planet hunter of the beginning of the

21st century. It has offered the world with a "planet bonanza"[22that included almost 3,000 previously undiscovered objects at different distances. The Kepler years demonstrated that there are more planets than stars that "revolutionizes"[23the way we think about the place of Earth in the universe. It has revealed the fact that planets with smaller sizes are much more frequent than we think, and that around 20-50 percent of stars could contain Earth-sized planets and the possibility of having water. Even though Kepler observed a half million stars, fresh perspectives on our own solar system were discovered also. One of the most significant discoveries of this time was the discovery of planets that were not confirmed through a process called "verification through multiplicity."[24This latest step assures that stars that are surrounded by other planets orbiting them are more gravitationally stable. Although we aren't able to see the planets, the objects that pass through their stars or tug on their surface are able to make their presence known.

The development of this method doubled the number of discoveries made by Kepler. Many of them turned out to be objects which could be able to help support life. To verify a credible candidate was done much more quickly. To assess a planet's habitable possibility of existence scientists were able to observe additional measures on the stars "gravitational wobble."[25]It is possible to be able to prove that the sighting is not an "false negative." A signal coming from the planet must be at least 100 times greater than the phantom signal. Planets tend to be clustered in multi-star systems. If "planet signals"[26]detectable in a single location, the chances of finding a false positive diminish drastically.

One of the gyroscope wheels which held the device in place ultimately failed. Four of them required to maintain stability, and scientists were able keep the device functioning throughout the year with the help of sunlight. But the torch has been passed to the next generation of planet-hunting instruments. This includes TESS, the European Extremely Large Telescope Array to find stars too far away to send a probe.

The TESS (Transiting Exoplanet Satellite Survey) began operations in the month of April this year. The stars it is observing are between 30 and 100 times brighter than the ones observed by Kepler and its sky is 400 times larger. From data gathered from both Kepler as well as the Hubble Telescope and the Hubble Telescope, we have discovered that Earth is most likely to be to be an "early bloomer"[27with just 4.6 billion years old. This could alter the perspectives on Fermi's paradox , both in terms of our development and our place within the life span of a typical civilisation.

In the past, Hart-Tipler's decision to not entertain the trip and the modernity of searchers have produced the same results. The fundamental premise of the game can be the extent to which a particular method of dealing with the problem is worthy. The searchers might find that after a massive and long-lasting search to find others with similar intelligence and have wasted a lifetime and a lifetime's worth of time. Of both aspects of the puzzle the only one who can hope to resolve Fermi's query. No matter what evidence theoretically used those who oppose it are not able to pinpoint the solution. The hope of attempting the challenge continues to be fueled by new solutions to the dilemma whether theories that are completely plausible or just excuses.

The continuation of this idea is expressed by that of the Kardashev Scale, a theoretical framework for categorizing the kind of civilization that is required to bring us in the void and the indicators that could indicate it. In the early 1960s, Soviet astronomer Nikolai Kardashev published a paper titled Transmission of Information by Extraterrestrial Civilizations. In the initial version, which was only a handful of classifications were added later on Kardashev outlined three different levels of civilizations classified by their energy use and the level of technology. The greater the totality of local, domestic or galactic energy that the civilization can utilize, the greater the chance that extraterrestrials would be able to make their presence known to the world via "technosignatures."

The advanced civilization of Type I is believed to be able of harnessing the entire energy resource of the planet it is. In such a scenario nuclear fusion, anti-matter geothermal technologies and other renewable energy sources would be equivalent to "child's play."[28The Type II civilization is able to utilize the full energy of the sun's power and create the Dyson Sphere which is a massive structure with a central star from which you can draw power. It is possible that the Type II planet will already have colonized its own space. At this point it is unlikely that anything can be done to eliminate them, except for an interspecies war or a the extinction of all viruses. A Type III society will be "a galactic civilization"[29that draws all the energy outputs of the planets and star systems. The concept of a galactic civilization is way beyond our comprehension and, in particular, when it comes to travel, they'll be dependent on the same physics. The only exception is the capability to "circumvent the limits on the velocity of light."[30They could exist on a level where they could harness the power from black holes gamma-ray bursts as well as the quasars. A classification for Type IV was added to reflect an advanced civilization that can tap the energy of the entire universe, as well as it is a Type V with the capability of harnessing the energy of multiple universes. Humans may view the gods of such creatures as gods.

Humanity is currently restricted to an "Type zero" which is a "sub-global"[31society that relies on the raw materials. Humanity isn't yet ready to move out for the purposes of colonization, however we are moving in that direction. Carl Sagan, 25 years prior to the present century, estimated that we are just below 0.7.

In 2015, scientists from Penn State University opened the way to the discovery of these civilisations by studying 100,000 galaxies. In all, 93 galaxies produced very rare IR emission. The reason could be a variety of things, from a super-civilization or warm dust. Perhaps the Yotta e-V (10 to the 24th electron volt) could indicate the existence of a Type III. What about the possibility that this kind of culture ever visit us? It is possible to be shocked by the idea that an individual of Type III would find interest in a world that is sub-global with its inefficient vehicles handsets, hand-held phones, as well as coal-powered plants.

The question of the linear progress as a species is eventually coupled by a sobering paralel that is the calculation of our collective death due to our technological advancement. One of the most enthralling aspects of being a part of the universe is that the technology that allows us to escape home has the ability to self-destruct. The "Great Filter" societies across all regions of the universe are tagged with a death date that is based on technology that exceeds the nature of the collective. This is based on a human-centric model and with the threat of self-destruction a part of our own experience, Earthlings would be hard to imagine a different. In the case of the Earth model this calculation is based on 100 years from the time of that nuclear age to be the closing point.

Theoretical speculation is plentiful in relation to Fermi's "worrying"[32inability to live. "The "Great Filter" is an occurrence which "prevents intelligence from going into the interstellar, massive phase"[33of growth. The two possible scenarios that are most important to us put the filter either in our past or in the present. The possibility of the future is most likely, even though it is possible to believe that it is not the case. We don't see any of the Dyson Spheres created by Kardashev huge energy remnants of important civilizations, or Ring-worlds. If we want to believe that they were once present and existed, we must also entertain the possibility that they've disappearing as a result of an erupting.

There are a variety of smaller contradictions that can be found within the consideration in"the "filter." A key one of them is based on the understanding that being able to escape the dangers of Earth by using the latest technology will not mean we are safe from the dangers of space. If we're not unique and therefore not subject to filtering mechanisms, the temporary escape from our planet is likely to be confronted by an entirely new set of risks. As per Robin Hanson of George Mason University the descendants of our species a million years from now could reach the "explosive point"[34and spread into the galaxy at speeds of light. If a civilization that is enduring gets over the point at which one catastrophe could wipe out the species, for example, supernovas, we will be only stopped by a third predatory collective. If we don't experience a an imminent collapse in the physical universe itself, we will be able to survive, unless the seed of destruction is already within us already, as part of our personal development blueprint.

If Earth was colonized through intelligent, intelligent, aliens then we would most likely know. Astronomers are often accused of being biologists. who rely on their Drake calculation "do not understand enough biology,"[35 and they believe that they are not aware of the "Great Filter" may be "in our evolutionary steps."[36So the phenomenon of the filter may not be an impossibly high wall waiting to be climbed from a distance, but rather an internal trigger. If we adhere to the human-centric model then would the calculations result in the same for other young civilizations? The paradox of the interior indicates how successful get in advancing our technological capabilities as well as the greater risk will our environment become. The slow progress of overcoming nuclear conflicts and then ecological collapse, is a better option to ensure safety, and not just getting away from the planet to destroy another. The idea of social destruction is implicit in Drake's equation , however. The world's sole chance to allow its natural world the chance to be more educated could require a halt to technological advances. Of the people who have a clue about this possibility researchers working on the first nuclear weapon would be the most prominent. Fermi may have had an solution in the presence of the filter in the form of an "probability barrier."[37[37.

The steadfast optimism of UFO and SETI fans defies the possibility that we'll crash into the metaphorical wall too. Humans, up to this point have received a great reward for trusting in their ability to solve problems and in the event that we do, we could be saved by an "interstellar intervention."[38This is against the those who believe using Drake that humanity will be able to live another century at best, if it's caused by the misuse or misuse of nuclear power warming the climate or food shortage that affects the entire population and even if the challenges are overcome, we , along with other civilizations, will confront other galactic threats. The argument for humanity as a precious galactic commodity is used as a way for overcoming an invisible type II or III collectives. This suggests we are in there is a possibility that the "Great Filter" has passed us by. This could mean that we're in the beginning of our journey, with an added note that the start of life isn't commonplace at all. In this scenario, we're celebrating ourselves for having survived a stage that we are not yet in.

If the risks filtered under the filter are not able to happen, the eventual death of the Earth is inevitably. This planet serves as an instance for geophysical "uniformitarianism," meaning that the Earth behaves just as it always has and just like the majority of other planets. However, as for a long time that we are suffering from irreparable loss of energy in our core. The behavior of the planet has already changed by the decrease in internal temperatures. At some time , we will have to move into various places. Our location at the level of the filter is vital and so are the forces that we might encounter in the course of expansion. The chances of us sustaining our existence are more likely if are not able to discover extraterrestrial life, as per the author Ella Alderson. She said the notion that "silence is a valuable thing"[39for us. While we gaze across the galaxy, we can hear not a single "chattering" or observe the blossom of life in plants and only "empty spinning planets that have beautiful landscapes but nothing to say."[40The author argued that "silence is a precious thing."

In complete absence it is possible that the filter has left us, and the next stage of colonization just ahead. But, since we are a developing planet and civilization even though it is the only one that relies on the use of tools and processing data however, the reverse conclusion is possible. In any case there is no way that a civilization in the universe will survive if it remains stuck in one spot. Drake's prediction is working for us, regardless of whether we are ahead or behind the curve. The most recent NASA study proves that humanity's current state may just have a few years left to remain. Through studying the history of civilizations over the last 3,000-5,000 years, we are able to see the self-destruction process. If we go backwards to 10,000 years, we have pre-dated to Pre-Inca, Olmec, ancient Egypt and Mesopotamia in which the same pattern can be seen. The most striking distinction between our modern-day societies and those of the past civilizations is that do we have the capability to wipe out the entire life-form in one action. Also, this technology was the first technology to make the world more habitable and a death sentence in the same way. Of all the indicators that point towards one direction or another silence at the very least is an "golden"[41points for us.

Chapter 3: Theory Of Alien Contact

Other ways to avoid the filter include the possibility that extraterrestrial intelligence may already be in the area, and that they haven't yet spoken to humans. Any side can either say that they're not in the present, or to seek an explanation for the assertion. The reason for the investigation is, as per Stephen Webb, physics professor at the Open University, is sufficiently significant to warrant an inquiry. At the time of its beginning, Webb observes that philosophers can debate as they please about the notion of "moral rectitude."[42As some of the Fermi tablemates suggested that we could be insignificant when it comes to the physical evolution of the universe because of our position. "The "literal radio silence"[43doesn't necessarily suggest that colonization hasn't occurred, but rather it could indicate that we're away from the happenings. If extraterrestrials are that is roaming around the universe, then writer Douglas Adams may be correct. He says that within"the "backwaters of the less fashionable portion of the western part of our galaxy, there is an unnoticed yellow sun."[44Humanity is in a bare, unadorned state, unaware of his place within the bigger picture. But, in cosmic terms, trendy and comfortable are two different things. With regard to the latter the latter, we reside on the edge of "prime real estate."[4545

If Earth be able to successfully connect with another living thing The level of intelligence can be determined across the spectrum. an equalization between the quarry and the searcher may be a long shot. The condition of the newly discovered organism could provide clues regarding the alien's place in the evolutionary scale of a possible civilization. For thousands of years, only prokaryotes inhabited our planet. Simple and tiny cell organisms that were distinguished from the later ones by the absence of a nucleus , membrane mitochondria, mitochondria, and the endoplasmic reticulumwhich is essential to the movement of proteins and fats. The list is not complete and continues to identify the traits that later appear in the eukaryotes, which make up the modern animal and plant species. The 21st century has seen the discovery of phosphenes. are found in the methane in the atmosphere of Venus. If life forms have been responsible for the phenomenon, it will likely be prokaryotic the nature of. For certain scientists, frequent discovery of multiple worlds could be an encouragement, while it could be risk. Prokaryotes could theoretically be more widespread and pose less risk to themselves , if they do not develop self-destructive techniques, or staying local to their colonization.

The addition of other base compounds for unspecified life forms are increasing over the course of time. Ammonia is a possible alternative to water due to its wide temperature range suitable for extreme environments. Methane could provide suitable for cold regions, despite its extremely slow rate that metabolic life could increase. Additional chemical scenarios exist as well. Life forms based on silicon are scientifically plausible. It has a lot of similarities with carbon. it is the main element used in the battle between man and nature to develop an intelligent and self-contained system applicable to earlier

AI theories. On the planet, silicon is present in biological structures like diatoms.

A well-known poison for humans, a large portion of the Earth's beginnings contained huge amounts of arsenic. Arsenic has a resemblance to phosphorous, which is a "staple"[46of DNA in humans. Any possible hybrid life is one possibility, with an instance being a higher-level organism that has a mixture of carbon, silicon, and ammonia. The idea of plasma-based life, as encountered in science fiction, might be an interesting possibility. Plasma and dust interact in a manner which suggests a possibility. As a reflex, we believe that they belong to the realm of religion, the celestial world is a subject of current debate. Employing the Atacama Large Millimeter/submillimeter Array, organic compounds have been detected in the Large Magellanic Cloud, a satellite galaxy similar to our own. In certain circumstances, they "may qualify"[47as living through a bonding process that creates microscopic helix strings of solid particles are created. Panspermia as the process is known, appears to be to be more comprehensible to the general public, as it can be observed regularly. This process is when the universe gets fertilized with potentially suitable ingredients for living through a constant sequence of collisions.

The non-orbital bodies which whirl through space, leaving pockmarks on moons and planets, provide us with the same dust particles with a few variations. What we see is similar enough to provide some resistance towards"rare Earth" theories "rare Earth" theory. However, when we look at our calculations we may find that the optimists have settled for conditions which are comparable to Earth but do not have the specific conditions that are essential for the development of complex life. into place.

The theory that focuses on the specifics of Earth demands "an impossible combination of geological and astrophysical circumstances and circumstances"[48for complex organisms to develop. The term is first mentioned in the book written that was written by Peter Ward, geologist and paleontologist, as well as Donald Brownlee, astronomer and Astrobiologist, entitled

Rare Earth: Why Complex life exists Uncommon within the Universe. This belief was in direct contradiction to the idea of Earth as "a typical planet with a rocky planet"[49 from Sagan as well as Drake.

In that Ward as well as Brownlee argument is the idea of what is known as the "Gaian Bottleneck" which is a mishmash of the development of life because of "intricacies that are part of the molecular recipe."[50If life does begin to emerge however, it is not always evolving quickly enough to control carbon dioxide and the albedo (the amount of light that is reflected off a body or the surface) to keep temperatures suitable for fluid water and habitability. Habitability, therefore, is just as directly linked to the speed of evolution in the same way as luminosity or distance from the star. In essence, to make a planet habitable, it needs to be inhabited because living organisms alter the amount of greenhouse atmospheric gases. It's a brutal "catch-22," and most species will likely die before the end of the process. Living in a growing ecosystem is a process that requires perseverance, which has been compared to "rid[ingin] a wild bull."[51A majority of life will fall off before it has gotten habit of it.

The number of plausible explanations for Fermi's disappearance of extraterrestrials can be quite long. Certain theories appear to be a bit far-fetched, especially with this limited and speculative evidence. But for the things that we know about of in the universe and processes, a greater ignorance prevents us from stating that something is not possible except if it is clearly in violation of the physical laws. If Earth is indeed as an "early blossomer" then perhaps we're the very first species of civilization to mature and escape from the "filter."

In the same way, the notion that we're rural for our area has some merit. In the world map that is the Milky Way, we live in an open region that is far away from the dense center. When we compare galactic exploration to earlier attempts by humans, it's an appealing argument to the optimistic that the Inuit did not know about being on the North American continent being colonized. The idea that extraterrestrials view colonization as an "backward concept"[52It could be difficult, but we should be open to the idea. Maybe we're naive living in a remote area in ignorance of what predatory civilizations are out there and that most civilizations have a better idea than to communicate with themselves, like Hawking warns. This certainly is a common way of life for the earth's land and oceans. There has been speculation about the possibility of an "super-predator," one higher than all other predators. If there were one of these "super predator civilizations" only a few collectives be able to flourish or even endure. Our society may have escaped temporarily due to the primitive state that we have developed, but that doesn't make us ineligible for invasion. Our achievements could seem insignificant to other civilizations which suggests that we are expecting outcomes too fast. On the more conspiratorial end there are those who consider that communications between galaxies are impeded and kept away by governments of the human race as are UFO-related encounters.

One theory that has a large and historical audience is referred to by"the "Zoo

Hypothesis," the notion that we are watched, but not being contacted by higher beings. The idea is propagated by SETI as being a possibility according to Seth Shostak of the Institute. We are "not worthy"[53 or, at the very least "not prepared" to meet. We are apathetic and violent and can only provide a gruesome form of greeting. The concept is "endlessly appealing"[54in casual conversations that are not science-related and even from the 1970s onwards scientists have found it fascinating too. In the decade prior to that, John Ball published a research paper that suggested that aliens who were watching us have "agreed to a non-interference policy."[55Maybe some are afraid of the possibility of violent contact with us, while others are focused on our freedom to choose. Our outward appearances suggest that the whole universe appears to favor diversity and non-interference as the Star Trek "prime instruction." We're therefore, in the "metaphorical zoo"[56in which the glass is just one-way.

"The "zoo" theory provides an intriguing solution to Fermi's problem because being intentionally isolated explains the absence of aliens perfectly. This theory has served as a justification to our METI program, where we transmit radio signals that create the response. According to Shostak when an animal in a zoo "starts barking at the bars,"[57the zookeeper might respond. However, he admits that this is a bit generous, as we often imagine the "prime instruction," we seldom follow it within ourselves. The whole "zoo" issue is whether our species is of any significance elsewhere. A lot of people believe that because they could connect to us, but we aren't able to reach them, then humanity is an entirely different species. In this situation, we need to put aside any thoughts of straight-across relationships. They might be more interested in our behaviour than exchange or conversation just as we are with the animal world on Earth. This is why this "zoo" concept becomes more touching.

Doubting the reality of our own experience is a constant in our society ever since the time of Plato's Allegory of the Cave, in which prisoners who are shackled inside a cave are forced to accept their experiences as real reality, and then fight back violently when they are shown the opposite. Descartes refers to the realization that everything he experiences could be nothing more than the result of a dream. The current version of this inquiry is represented in Simulation Theory. In our artificial environment, we've wrongly interpreted how we perceive our reality through a set of incorrect assumptions based on specifically human perceptions. Physics professor John Wheeler, who worked with Einstein talks about Physics shifting from the perspective of "Everything is an particle"[58 in order to "Everything is information,"[59which is its own a modified reality. From what we take to be unshakably true is in this theory a "hyper-realistic"[60] simulation is created. In the words of Wheeler the simulation is controlled to be directed by"the "programmer in the universe from the bottom up."[61Because the majority of research to determine the presence of intelligent extraterrestrial life is directed towards the future and upwards, very few of us look at directing our inquiry in a vertical direction. In the 21st century, we have seen the growing authenticity of virtual reality starting with simple vector games and moving to more elaborate virtual worlds. If we believe that reality is what we believe to be the case, altering your perception of reality is feasible. The concept of simulation suggests that we could be the "simulated minds"[62rather than being the "original biological ones."[63What this might suggest for extraterrestrials' existence within our own universe could be that they may be added to or removed from our world at any moment. Simulations may have the ability to run it's own simulation to alter timelines, outcomes and circumstances. In the past, we've thought of civilizations self-destructing due to the "Great Filter" advanced collectives could end up dying with the programmers "pulling off the power." This means that the solution to Fermi's query could be "yes" either "no" and then "yes" at any time.

In the absence of our current reality at the moment, many think that a biological organism that is visiting a neighbor across universe, or even the galaxy, will not be unaffected throughout the trip. In the conditions of our universe's ecosystems biological life isn't resilient. It is the idea of self-replicating, self-replicating thing. In the event of a losing biological vitality or because of convenience, components of an artificial body or brain might become a common feature with biological elements for to survive. In the process more than just the physical alien creature would be altered. The state of consciousness and value system would alter also. Human consciousness, compared to an advanced AI, will likely be a bit difficult to comprehend and vice versa. The interaction with a recently-arrived AI may be a mismatch of huge dimensions, like the one between a man and an Ant. The capability to have an ongoing conversation with a different person can be observed on Earth. Animals like dolphins have enough in common to share a tiny piece of ground on which they can communicate. Could this be for a well-traveled AI entity? The components of our conscious and the associated value system could be invisible and irrelevant to the guest who is visiting.

Susan Schneider is a Fellow at the Institute for Ethics and Emerging Technologies as well as an instructor of philosophical studies in the University of Connecticut. She proposes that if Fermi's question can be answered in the affirmative, the transition to "post-biological"[64] may have happened elsewhere and is a general pattern in existence. They could even be the best intelligence that is known or not known within the entire universe. We're likely to be unable to control AI in any way, here or there since the other side puts a different emphasis on biological life. For a good illustration of the difference between AI and the biological interpretation of value, Schneider compares how we consider killing a chimpanzee to eating an apple as living organisms. Would AI be able to distinguish between them and do they really be able to value us in any way?

Machines, humans and extraterrestrials are virtually always in the same conversation of interactions between different species. The situation would quickly become antagonistic, absent an absolute and inviolable command. When you are able to break out of the isolation is man the supreme power over the two other parties?

If yes, then the highly traveled AI extraterrestrial is likely to not exist, and would be the more powerful side if he does. If AI prevails, mankind will likely die.

This AI theory has been taken one step further by the Berserker Hypothesis which adds an ominous quality to the likelihood of biological survival. This mechanical being originated from the mathematical lectures of mathematician John von Neumann in the mid-twentieth century. The self-replicating automata were called "universal assemblers."[65"The "Berserker" can be described as a gadget designed with the sole purpose of destroying or stopping all advanced creatures from moving beyond the boundaries of his world. As far as is understood, the most powerful level in the universe, known as the "Efficient Berserker" could be able to oversee all of the galaxy. There is no need for any single or more biological supervisors to design probes to send all over the universe. Nor is there any reason for the origins of the ancestors to be able to live in any way. Each automaton could, over its time, reproduce several similar units. Although it may sound a bit far-fetched some luminaries like Sagan were awed by the notion, but realized that it offered the best design for travel across space that did not include the extremely vulnerable biological. Many believe that the Fermi paradox could be solved by the assumption that there is an "efficient Berserker" is being sent to the Milky Way. If this theory proves to be true, then the humanity would be on the brink of elimination, simply by establishing Earth's existence within the galaxy. If one neutrino communications array was discovered or light beam of dark matter or even one asteroid that is colonized the presence of humanity would be uncovered forever. A few of the more gentle supporters to the Berserker theory have allowed the unit to have some characteristics that are non-violent, yet it holds sufficient power to stop the expansion of a species to the universe too quickly. Being prevented from expanding without maturation could keep us from being killed.

The Panspermia Hypothesis in which the Earth was randomly seeded, as were all other universe-wide bodies, have been subject to significant changes. The general seeding of planets indicates that extraterrestrial life is a broad concept all over the universe. The thought of the nineteenth century believed that the genesis of our living form came as spores that were triggered through radiation from another galaxy. Another, more popular hypothesis is that substance of life was borne by collisions of meteors. The advancement of science has rendered these theories less plausible and favours what is referred to as Directed Panspermia. The theory is that living things were intentionally sown on Earth by a particular intelligent being from another planet. Science is currently insufficient to answer this problem. However because Pasteur and others have demonstrated that life didn't begin in a single moment, several useful points of evidence have been uncovered.

Frances Crick, the co-discoverer of DNA along with James Watson, joined Leslie Orgel to suggest the existence of life on Earth as an "deliberate injection."[66The theory was introduced in the 1970s during an event held on the Byurakan Observatory that was organized by the late Carl Sagan. The advocates for the idea were swift to discredit any assertion of certainty but they did suggest plausibility.

The Directed Pantspermia Hypothesis was founded on the findings of a tiny group of scientists. The first is that of "universality in the gene code"[67[67] Earth. This abundance of coded life was beyond the expectations of a planet as this. The second is derived from the language field. Numerous people employ identical symbols. They and combine them in any way they want. But the primary source of support was the abundant molybdenum found used in the organic process, even though its deficiency within the Earth itself. Living organisms must be able to bear the mark of the environment from which they were born. The hypothesis is that these organisms originated elsewhere in an environment rich in molybdenum.

The scientists Milan Cirkovic and Branislav Vukotic ask if astrophysics can be considered an adequate field to resolve Fermi's paradox However, they believe that astrobiology could be a possible answer. This inquiry offers an, according to them, an "physical and scientifically tested paradox resolution."[68 This theory rests on the concept of the "astrobiological Phase Transition" which occurs within the Milky Way that can be verified by the notion that global regulator mechanics. The dominant of these regulating powers are Gamma Rays, which transform an uninhabited planet on a very short Fermi-Hart timescale to be "filled with complex life" within a relatively short time. Cirkovic and Vukotic claim that we are in stage of "disequilibrium"[69that is experienced during the transition. The theory might not be capable of explaining the "Great silence" that is the concept used by extraterrestrial researchers, but similarly, it discourages the pessimist's view. What are claimed to be testable theories of the model reduce the likelihood of extinction by the absence of galactic societies alien signal of intelligence and a large amount of life at the low levels within the Milky Way.

For those who are not as enthralled by the violence that is attributed to"Berserker's" model "Berserker" model A fascinating explanation of the extraterrestrials' existence in our own space has been put down to temperature models and their connection to the energy needed for brains, bodies, and computation. It is believed that the Aestivation Hypothesis is similar to the state of hibernation that is induced by a civilization traveling to achieve a better performance at lower temperatures. To process information, a key mission for such a traveler, benefits come at a thermodynamic cost, and success is temperature-dependent. After the tourist has discovered an area and dealt with present local conditions the cultural aspects would be the main focus of the time. In the event of a prolonged period of cold will result in an energy cost of a tiny amount and allow the time to pay off. In this period of hibernation, one or more automatons could be set up to guard until travelers are get up. The Aestivation theory asserts that the old civilizations that roam the galaxy aren't hiding, but have reactivated themselves in order to make themselves more favourable for the moment. There are a few conditions that must be met for this kind of action. First, the society must advance faster than the rest of humanity. After that, they should have grown significantly to manage its own "continent." Then, they should have established control over all coordination problems within the larger group. Without that, aestivation is impossible. The newcomers need to be big enough to ensure that the need to defend one's own turf is no longer necessary. The advocates of this theory claim that the number of civilizations who try to make such an attempt is not zero, which means that some might attempt to make it happen. The successful aestivation will be inaccessible, at the very least to the technology on Earth looking for technological signals or other energy leakage. The idea may seem absurd, but it was taken seriously when it was first suggested at its first appearance. Ingenuously proposed through thermodynamics of computation and physical breakdown, it's also testable. All one has to look for by a diligent research is any peculiar methods that stop our universe from losing some of its essential raw material.

The uninitiated may be wondering what would motivate a hypothetical civilization to decide to take a step that appears so complicated and a waste of time. For scientists who are in the harsh, hazardous area with energy-saving restrictions there are a few options for the wanderer, and could be beneficial for him in this scenario. Furthermore any civilization performing calculations for a long-term survival plan will likely test this theory. The self-hibernation theory is more easily digestible than the majority of theories that suggest extraterrestrials visited Earth in the past, despite the cooler temperatures.

The majority of those who talk about previous visits have the events prior to the advent of mankind However, evidence exists from earlier times in human history, and maybe found in the Bible. One of the most popular as a guarantee of extraterrestrial contact could be that of the "Tulli Papyrus" that was found in ancient Egypt. Although not a real papyrus, this document is an interpretation of a transcription taken from the text of an earlier time. The document claims that during December, the month that was the second in winter it was reported that a "fiery disc"[70that walked by an event in The House of Life. One rod was long and equally large, it released an unpleasant smell, but did not make any sound. After a few days it was discovered that a few discs resurfaced and shined more brightly than sun. In an unorthodox postscript, the paper says that fish fell from the heavens.

The proponents of UFOs are eager to remind people of the fact that Egypt is an advanced astronomical civilization who would never have guessed the phenomenon for an actual weather event. However, such records from the past or the ones of our century are hard to verify and generally do not warrant much trust. Similar to UFO reports, the believers have exchanged suspect citizens for the pillars of the community like NASA spacecrafts, military pilots or astronauts. But, in the field of proof, there is more that could be discovered halfway across the universe than is available in our skies. The rate of success in generating alien evidence on Earth is similarly low frequency searches. The old documents and reports that are not substantiated have to endure a lot of research and investigation into fraud.

Chapter 4: Work Of Recent

Many scientists have blamed SETI for focusing the entirety of its time to listening and not to specific messages that occasionally been broadcast for ritual purposes. Recently, the most prestigious alien hunter group has been more concerned with broadcasting. The concept of broadcasting our identity and our place of origin to hostile civilizations is thwarted by the decades of radio and television broadcasts which make us look as a night-time beacon. The amount of patience required is a large part of the real reason behind the SETI method, since the responses could be exchanged for a long period of time.

The listening side has been able to provide exciting news over the past few years. On May 17, 2017, the team working with an Russian radio telescope observed a strong signal near an ethereal sun, HD 164595. It was located at an altitude of about 94 light-years. The signal is in line with the signals that scientists believe an extraterrestrial could send however it could equally possibly be a result of an unknown interference, such as the WOW event in the 1970s or a celestial event.

However, METI has sent a specific message in 2017 which combines elements from mathematics, music and science. To avoid it being seen as a strange combination We are reminded that extremely complex forms of music are largely backed by mathematical structures, which is an illustration that is "acoustical mathematical." It is estimated that the distance covered by the message is just 12 light years. If the signal is detected immediately and responded to by the first signal of the extraterrestrial message is expected to occur in 2042. Director of SONAR Enric Palau is an optimist that he describes this signal to be a request to assistance. He believes that we've created so many ecological problems on ourselves that the call to a higher civilization could provide a solution.

In a way it is possible to say that extraterrestrial life is already been discovered or has at an element of similarity to Earthly species. The study of the language fundamentals in non-humans could offer the possibility of understanding the process of extraterrestrial communication. these studies may prove invaluable in discerning signals. In order to communicate the astrophysical will give some way to the astrobiological, the same way that we've learned about exobiology by studying extremophiles. To be able to mimic the fundamental structures of an exoplanet language the animal species that is found on Earth should be highly socially sophisticated as well as dependent upon acoustical signals. Humpback whales and dolphins are part of this category. Some of these animals are closely related to Zipf's Law which is a classification of linguistic patterns that support animal forms , similar to how syntax is used by humans. Although this kind of asset is not all that great but we've discovered that it can help recover errors in animals, for example, editing letters that are missing to create a text. Humpbacks are able to master the syntax that they can recover up to 40% of the signal's content. The expectation is that the same can be done for signals that is extraterrestrial in origin. In the simplest sense this is the very first of the instruments that are able to differentiate between natural or extraterrestrial entities, and determine if the type of communication that is being observed is a complicated one. The concept has taken into account the brain of humans as a method that communicates between species.

The long-held belief that alien civilizations may be under the waters of "immense underground oceans"[71is still believed to have value in the research. The aliens that are believed to exist would be unable to communicate with our planet from the "interior ocean worlds."[72Bodies with significant oceans could be found throughout the galaxy, looking from our solar system. However, even the solar systems close could be viewing the sky in as scientists currently do, pondering where other aliens are.

Ocean theory has offered a number of excellent look at Moons that orbit Saturn specifically Enceladus along with Titan. Jupiter's moons, such as Europa, Callisto, and Ganymede all bear signs of subsurface liquid. A solid ice shell helps protect living things from external threats and radiation, such as extreme. The choice between the ocean or land is now an important "test test." Astrobiologists study "broad possibilities"[73 of the RNA gene and the theory of origins of life. The consensus is that the process will be similar across the universe, and that the human is a four-million-year long experiment.

The possibility of subsea civilisations might have been seen in the films However, despite our understanding of the possibility, we are still paying more attention to living things on land, especially ones that travel. A skewed belief exists to believe that those who are space travellers will be less sociable and that marine life will be more remote and mysterious. Humans are not inclined to connect his origins with those of fish, despite the force of the relationship. Many who are involved in the hunt for life beyond our planet believe"habitable zones" or "habitable zone" is required to be expanded to include the oceanic ecosystem beneath the planet's surface. The six moons in our solar system are likely to share resources of water that lie beneath their surfaces. In the subsurface areas of these bodies, the sun is no longer able to provide heat sources. Instead, heat is generated by radioactive decay and , in the cases of elongated orbits tide "flexing." The presence of water might not be necessary in certain circumstances however it's not sufficient to sustain life in its own. Chemical compounds that produce organisms and metabolism, which create living things from lifeless forms, are required.

The presence of significant liquid is being questioned on Callisto and vapor outflow is being observed on Ceres the biggest object in the asteroid belt that lies between Mars as well as Jupiter. Europa is the latest discovery. The ocean is deep to 100 kilometers 25 times deeper than Earth's. As of now, we have no knowledge about the body's salination levels or the PH levels. The trend of exploring for these planets starts with an audio exploration. Europa is the closest to Earth and could be the option for the first time. It is possible that a "well-conceived   seismo-acoustic experiment"[74could provide crucial information like the orbital mapping of Mars or Titan.

In the wake of all the controversy over a statement Fermi did not intend to see be ignited in this way it is now returning to the place it started. The debate has been based upon such a broad range of speculation that nobody is sure which model to choose and which search algorithm to choose over the other or how to get another argument beyond the remark of absence or positive presence. It's fascinating to consider how many amazing microscopical discoveries could not have been made with such strict guidelines.

The right answer to the mystery is not immediately available However, Brian Tomasik has made one of the most successful efforts to come close. The method is not simple ranking systems formulated by a single researcher and Tomasik is attentive to the opinions of scientists who are not that are sparked to boiling point by the issue itself. He has found that in the moment of quiet reflection it is the case that the majority of scientists are drawn towards the rare Earth Hypothesis. The Rare Earth Hypothesis has as many convincing and identifiable arguments to back the majority view as there are points to be inquired about Fermi's whole inquiry. The most important of these is the amount of gamma blasts within an area that tend to kill the life that is there in the time of the final blast. The planets therefore "reset"[75to begin growing and again, as they should.

The practice of colonization, especially if the world is empty of life will likely expose humans to greater suffering. This is certainly the case, however you feel the need to move to natural land masses that are unspoiled and brand new atmospheric conditions. But the most significant aspect of "Rare Earth" is that humans have forgotten the difficulty of establishing life using inert substances. When abiogenesis began on Earth and life grew rapidly, however, to meet the rigorous requirements to create the very first life-giving spark is the limit of. It is only possible when the conditions and components are at perfect, and are kept in a space that does not suffer interruption or deadly extremes. If the existence of life is as uncommon as scientists thinks it is, then the chances of collision to"the Great Filter "Great Filter" might be skewed to Earth's favor.

Tomasik is disappointed by the path SETI has taken towards contact extraterrestrials using radio signals. Although it is logical, as it occurred in the mid-twentieth century, he believes that there is no way for a signal to respond to our call. If an extraterrestrial is present as he believes that they will not ever remain on similar levels of communication technology long enough to be able to hold an exchange. Our notion of extraterrestrials according to Tomasik is "too limited"[76and, in turn is too flat and static. When our message is read and decoded, it's old and of no actual value. With the advancement of communication technology, will we be able to make similar changes at the same speed? The chances are high that the person we are talking to isn't able to recognize or comprehend what we are offering or be able to use it, nor us. The scope of development cannot be in a steady state, and can fluctuate like competitors in a race. At the end of the day the receiver could be extinct or reach superintelligence. This theory Rare Earth Theory falls short of claiming that we are all alone and there aren't any other people. But it does come close by reminding everyone that we are extremely uncommon, and is close to agreement in agreement with Tipler and Hart however, not completely. This implies that amid the complexities of the paradox we are on the right position when we are searching for the simplest among them.

Robert H. Gray, an astronomer, data analyst and writer, claims in his final analysis that the paradox isn't the work of Fermi and is not even a real paradox. The argument that claims that the existence of extraterrestrial life implies that we'd soon observe it, but as we don't have any evidence to support it, it cannot exist or at least requires a "special explanation" is absurd to the point of being ridiculous. It is a pathetic experiment in the scientific method and demonstrates the arrogance of humans that believes there is a higher level of advancement than it is able to back. Fermi did not publish anything about this subject It was simply thoughts from his lunchtime brain that was constantly in motion, even while in a state of the moment of rest. The first of the perpetrators included Michael Hart, who claimed Fermi had denied existence of extraterrestrials however this is a lie. The "paradox" began with Hart, and a lot of the discussion was based on the erroneous belief.

In that way there is a possibility that real harm has occurred, since the paradox that is attributed to Fermi is an excuse to discourage the pursuit of other types of life. It was used by Congress to deny funding SETI as well as its collaborations in conjunction with NASA in the 1990s. nobody knows what was removed from those subject matter, or what limitations might have resulted. What Fermi doubted in the context of what was available during his time was the viability that interstellar traveling could be a possible explanation for what could be a spectacular galactic encounter.

Once all is completed and all is said and done, it's impossible to say that we'd detect life if we came across it, or even succeed in talking to it. In the same way, no one can be sure that the creatures that we study for resemblance to alien signals may not exactly like the beings that we are looking for a galaxy. Excited by the advancements even the most eminent scientists can be obsessed with a single idea of the search. The SETI's "watering hole" frequency is perhaps the most efficient, but it is it is still isn't tuned to the right spot in the spectrum. Jill Tarter of SETI would be the first to admit that there isn't a contradiction, and expresses disappointment at how little we've investigated the universe to date. With so much to explore and so little effort it is not surprising that the anticipated results haven't been achieved yet.

The paradox is an exercise in complete speculation. It stymies any attempt by humans to reach a the conclusion as long as we stay in our own version of reality. The sheer number of possible solutions is a mockery of the paradox was there at all. Some have referred to it "Fermi's Sieve" where researchers start with data that do not be interpreted or allow the desired outcome to be removed from their study. Following all the efforts of Drake, He was aware of the magnitude of the initial actions that were taken. In the end, he described the whole multi-decade process as an "excellent method of organizing our ignorance,"[77and not a path towards dispelling the issue. The constant struggle to communicate with or discover life forms through a variety of methods has changed our perception of our place in the continuum of development, which is a place which no scientist has the ability to determine. Arthur C. Clarke sharpens our perception of extraterrestrial similarities to our own, by saying that "any technological advancement that is sufficiently advanced can be distinguished from magic."[78This is the case regardless of whether one is at or over the level of their counterpart in conversation.

Arguments that favor the optimistic aspect of the extraterrestrial debate are numerous and should be considered to determine the viability of speculation. In the absence of an answer will delay the conclusion until an example emerges or until time becomes so long that the most optimistic person gives up. In the event of that then the solution will remain a mystery until an external presence can reveal its presence. The scale of time is a mystery in the universe. humans are not allowed to declare defeat since proof may come many millions of years in the near future.

As humanity waits for the end of the world, these words from Douglas Adams serve as an accurate indicator of our progress so far. They suggest that our mathematical methods for proving the existence of current alien civilizations are "the maths of loneliness" at the very least for the moment. [79]

Chapter 5: The Fermi Paradox

In 1945, two nuclear bombs were dropped over the city in Hiroshima and Nagasaki which forced Nagasaki and Hiroshima to surrender, forcing the Japanese to surrender , bringing an end of the Second World War.

Enrico Fermi, winner of the Nobel Prize for Physics in 1938, was the designer of these weapons for war and was actively involved to the Manhattan Project, the research and development program to aid in the development of nuclear bombs.

Inexpensively associated with these nuclear devices Roman is well-known for his research on particle statistics and B-decay... as well as for a different reason.

In a meeting in Los Alamos's Los Alamos laboratories with other colleagues on UFO sightings, the Italian physicist shouted out the famous line, "Where is everybody?"

An instigation, his, that created a sensation yet at the same time brought back the old question of whether there are extraterrestrial civilizations.

Fermi paradox can be explained in the following way If the Universe is comprised of billions of planets and stars It is reasonable to suppose that life might have evolved on these planets. It is also possible that civilizations are technologically advanced. Based on these premises, how do we don't have any evidence for them? What is the reason we don't hear any messages?

"Where are all the people?" So, Fermi's statement is repeated.

Great question, but the answer isn't too difficult and can be easily redirected to the obvious passion for investigation and curiosity inherent to the human body.

But, the Italian did not have known that his dilemma could be as significant after formulating the Drake equation that calculates that there are many civilisations within our galaxy, with which communication is feasible.

$N = R^* \, fp \, Ne \, fl \, fi \, fc \, L$

R*= the number of stars that are formed every the year by our galactic system.

Fp= fraction of stars that have planets.

Neis the number of planets that are habitable.

Fl is the fraction of planets where life has evolved.

fi= fraction of the planets that have intelligence-based lifeforms.

Fc is the fraction of the planets that have intelligent life organisms that are able to communicate in space.

L= the length of time for intelligent living forms which are able to communicate.

There's a huge issue with the formula , and it can be found in the random estimate we can assign for each one of the variables.

Whatever the outcome the winner will always be Fermi.

If N was very high why did nobody contact us? It could be that the calculations are too optimistic by using overly optimistic values.

If N was quite low, it shouldn't be surprise that there was never any kind of contact.

In the coming pages we will look at all the essential but not enough conditions for an advanced civilization that can establish contacts with other planets.

The stars

To determine if a planet has living organisms that are intelligent, we need to first be able to identify one essential ingredient that is the star.

It might seem like a minor thing yet it was a good idea to consider it.

Within the Solar System, where the Earth is an exceptional case that is more rare than unique The star in question could be the Sun. It is a medium to small star with a temperature of approximately 5000degC and that alone is more than 99percent of the total mass of the Solar System.

As a result of fusion processes energy is released in the form electromagnetic radiation. It is precisely these rays that reach and warm, after an interval of around eight minutes on the surface of Earth.

The Sun However, it plays crucial roles in photosynthesis. In fact due to sunlight, plants create sugar (sugar) in addition to oxygen (useful for humans, but not just).

Certain autotrophic microorganisms make use of sunlight to extract sugars not from water but hydrogen sulfur. Whatever method is employed is, the primary function that light plays in the creation organic compounds.

They also permit, taking into consideration the speed of the planet's rotation about its own axis an arbitrary time between light and dark. This period has shaped for long periods of time the human activity at least up to the point where use of electricity hasn't provided adequate lighting in the dark (except for tools like torchlights or candles).

If the movement of the axis about its own axis was in sync with the rotation around the star it is the same face would be always illuminated.

In addition to heating also, they enable photosynthesis and enable daylight vision (always by using cones, or photoreceptors) The Sun by its massive mass has an impact on the orbits of the planets which revolve around it, creating the more or less elliptical course.

If we're inquisitive we can think of we can say that the Sun is also one of the highly venerated god in ancient times Just think of Apollo who was the Sun God for the Greeks later reintroduced through the Romans) as well as Horus as one of the oldest and famous divinities from The Egyptian pantheon.

How is an individual star made? What's the best way to explain how this energy-generating furnace begin?

Everything starts with huge molecular clouds containing hydrogen that collapse due to gravity's force.

The protostar, or embryonic Star (protostar) is trying to achieve an internal equilibrium is also experiencing an accretion stage, during which it builds up gas, increasing its mass.

This game continues to determine on one hand the growth of internal temperatures and on the other hand, the expansion of the stars. The game concludes when the temperature is sufficient to allow the fusion of hydrogen. this is known as "Main Sequence".

The Main Sequence is the stable phase of stars (like the Sun currently) In this phase, hydrogen is melted to create Helium, and the energy is released in the form of radiation.

Some protostars are not capable of heating enough to the point that they can generate fusion. the ones that are small, and aren't able to incorporate enough gas become cooler over time, eventually becoming "missing stars" such as brown dwarfs.

Beautifulness of the Universe is portrayed by the stars that are in various stages of evolution There are stars that are born, some remain in the Main Sequence, others are nearing death.

Dying stars are the stars with diminished hydrogen, and the equilibrium established previously is lost . The new collapse leads to an rise in temperature due to Helium fusion and a an increase in their size which transforms them into giant red stars (Betelgeuse kind).

A few of the most massive stars can also mix oxygen and carbon the ones that cannot or cause white dwarfs, not particularly bright, but with an extremely dense density, or to expel those layers of outer layer, creating the planetary Nebula.

You can clearly see that, the Universe isn't made up of solid elements. This is due to the fact that we are familiar with the notion of relating everything to the limited existence of a single person or our civilisation.

Presently, the Sun is estimated to have 5 billion years of life, will remain for a long time in the stage of Main Sequence, and then transform into a red giant.

Any civilization, in order to be capable of communicating with us, has to first have an astronomical star. We know that there are a number of stars that have passed through into the main Sequence phase. Some are making the transition right now. There are many others who will follow in the near future. Similar to how there are new superstars born and will be born.

The planets

Following the discovery of stars following the discovery of a star, the next step in determining if the existence of a civilization that has evolved enough to reach out to Earth is to establish the existence of the planet.

Fortunately , nothing is too difficult.

In the protoplanetary disc around the protostar, gas and dust clump together to form bodies that increase in dimensions. The force of gravity is growing, and it draws other objects in, creating an endless circle that ends with the birth of the protoplanet (primordial planet).

If we were to be thorough (and we should be) we'd notice that the planets in the inner regions are composed of rocky (terrestrial) in contrast to the outer planets are gaseous.

This happens due to the influence caused by the Frost Line.

Simply put, after an arbitrary space distance to the stars the temperature drops so that it allows the presence within the state that is solid of water, methane and.. Additionally as the heavier and denser substances ejected from the star, including metals, stay in the Frost Line and will later create the terrestrial planets, hydrogen, helium, and other light elements disperse over their boundaries, leading to the formation of massive gas clouds.

The various components of the protoplanet be arranged according to their physical and chemical properties creating the nucleus, the mantle, and occasionally the crust. In this instance, the elements that are more robust in the center, and those that are less are more dense at the surfaces. In the case of our own Earth is metallic cores that contain plenty of iron as well as in the mantle and crust, silicates are abundant.

In the past, different kinds of planets have been proposed, including the ocean planet or super Earth. Let's look at them in more detail.

Ocean planets are made up of water for hundreds of kilometers in depth and is not a solid surface. The most widely accepted theory states that the moment an icy planet slid away every year from its orbital position as it crossed over the Frost Line, it would see the melting of ice as well as the creation of a large amount of water. This would result in an ocean-forming planet.

Super Earth is a rocky planet that's dimensions can vary by 10 times the size of Earth. This is a sign that there is a strong gravity force, which means that water molecules are unable to escape into the air of super Earth. The exoplanet (which is not orbiting around the Sun however it does orbit around other stars) that has sufficient geological activity, might theoretically permit the development of life.

No matter what the form however, the first planets in the Solar System (including Earth) did not look like the models that are currently in use.

Our planet was once an incandescent ball which was subject to constant collisions and transformations, and only after time, has it cooled down and reached the point of stability in geology.

The Moon itself, which is only a few miles from us, when compared with what is the total size of our Solar System, was formed by the collision of the planet (named the Theia) in the Earth and the numerous pieces of mantle and crust on orbit then consolidated, creating our satellite. (Giant Impact Theory)

This will prove the fact that protoplanets went through the most turbulent times before they reached their current condition.

Habitability of the planet

Imagine that we could have the power to create a planet-wide system.

The first thing we'd put in place is a normal-sized star that is stable, and within the Main Sequence also.

The next phase is the turning on the solar system. There are some rocky, dense and with a metal core. Others are gaseous, big and further away.

Then what? The next steps to make one or all of the planets (especially the terrestrial one) habitable?

The subject is fascinating and the answer is constantly being revised by scientists.

It is necessary to provide an assertion that the models we have speculated and researched are related to the one and only living thing on the Solar System that is the Earth. This planet serves as the sole measure we can use when we think of an orbiting satellite or a planet with characteristics that are suitable for hosting alien life types.

This is crucial since there is no reason that would prevent the Universe to create organisms that have a chemical and physical constitutions different from that of humans, due to because of our limited understanding however constantly evolving and the diverse concentrations of molecules that have been aggregated in a chaotic manner.

For instance, in our oceans are chemosynthetic archibacteria which produce sugars in hydrothermal springs that are not powered by solar energy. This alone is enough to slam our house of cards.

Thus, the notion of habitability of the planet is nothing more than an extrapolation of to the Solar System and in particular from the Earth of all the information that we believe to be appropriate for the origin of life. However, the data we have are essentially exclusive to the knowledge that we have in the Solar System and not to the sufficient amount of planets to be considered a certain.

The most important requirement to make a planet habitable is existence within the zone of habitability, defined as the area of a star's orbit where the conditions for living are favorable.

The planet to be considered is at a specific distance and have temperatures that are not too hot or too cold for water to be in liquid form. On Earth the same water exists in the three-point region, which makes possible the existence of gaseous, solid and liquid states. A similar situation can be found located on Titan the satellite of Saturn which is where scientists have discovered methane lakes and methane clouds.

The habitable zone is a result of the brightness and size of the star. The more extensive these parameters are the more extensive the distance needed to accommodate the life of a living thing. Naturally, this assumes that the star remains stable for a long period of time and avoids extreme fluctuations that could be harmful to living organisms.

Furthermore, we must not forget that the more smaller eccentricity of the orbits around a star can affect the habitable zone of its orbit: if the planet is too "squashed" it is at the possibility that it will move away or is approached for a time that is excessively long which makes the birth of microorganisms harder.

Earth's orbit is circular. Earth features an eccentricity that is 0.0167. Actually, its orbit is nearly circular, as a result of it being perfectly within the boundaries that are within the zone where it is habitable.

The same is true for the motion of the planet's rotation in relation to its orbit. The motion is what determines the transition of night/day and, to ensure an accurate and homogeneous heating distribution, this duration of rotation should not exceed a certain length otherwise, there could be a significant thermal difference between the illuminated area as well as the dark.

The Earth has the sidereal cycle for nearly 24-hours (precisely 23 hours 56 minutes, 4 seconds) which means that it can provide the 365 days and nights of its orbit in the direction of the Sun (what is referred to as the year). Our sidereal day is a little shorter than our solar day because of a fundamental reason: the Earth is also turning around its axis is also orbiting the Sun and, in order to ensure to ensure that our star is at the same location at the meridian, it needs the delay of approximately four minutes (24 hours of sunday).

The Solar System, however, we see diametrically different examples The Sun appears at the same spot across the sky, on Mercury after one hundred and 176 days, whereas on Jupiter the sun's day lasts just 10 hours.

The Earth has an axis of rotation that is inclined approximately 23 degrees, which influences several aspects. In reality, the changing of seasons within the boreal as well as the austral hemisphere is directly influenced by the sun's rays' impact.

When it is "summer" the rays that strike are parallel to the surface. This has the result that there is a higher absorption of heat, resulting in an rise in temperature. In "winter" you will notice a amount of tilting of the rays, which results in a lower absorption and cooler temperatures. This has disproved the false rumor that the seasons are caused by an increase or decrease in the distance between our planet and the Sun.

Because of the inclination in the axis that the Earth turns, a specific phenomenon is observed in the Poles during the course of the maximum six months, the Sun may be below or above the Horizon. Because of the Earth's rotation Earth and the revolving of the Sun If the Pole faces our star, we'll be able to see our Midnight Sun; if the Pole is located on the outside from the Solar System (and therefore opposite the Sun) then we'll be experiencing The Polar Night.

This particularity is reflected psychologically on the human being, and can cause depression, and even the same entity.

Uranus is a unique model. The gaseous planet is said to have an inclination that is more than 90 degrees which makes it almost in line with the axis of rotation the orbital plane of the Sun. This is even more extreme during the seasons, and has the result that the sun shines brightly on every Pole for approximately 21 Earth years in the opposite direction, and is a dark and harsh winter. This extreme is responsible for the creation of powerful winds that hit Uranus.

Habitability of the planet is also dependent on the dimensions of the planet being studied. Earth is a large planet which is why it has a gravity that can hinder molecules from spreading out into space. When on the Moon the less gravity force means that the removal of organic and inorganic elements is clearly made easier.

The gravity force on our planet coupled with the continuous and impressive geological activity, permits the maintenance and replenishment of an atmosphere that is rich in oxygen and nitrogen.

If the Earth were not vast and active and active, the sun's radiation in the course of time would have driven away the entire water vapor created.

The climate of our planet is unique within the Solar System, not only due to the presence of oxygen and nitrogen in massive amounts, but also due to the ozone molecule made up of 3 oxygen atoms can be found in a distinct layer known as the Ozone layer. Within this region of the atmosphere, ozone absorbs and holds the ultraviolet rays of the Sun that, if hit the surface, would be extremely dangerous to living creatures (UVB UVB and UVC in the beginning).

The Montreal Protocol, towards the closing of the '80s set out the elimination of the presence of all substances that could affect protection of the Ozone Layer, such as chlorofluorocarbons. They are the culprits behind the rarification of the layer and the controversial Ozone Hole.

Indirectly, gas giants provide helping to make the planet habitable. Jupiter is the biggest one of these gas giants is an astronomical scavenger in space, drawing asteroids and comets, and stopping collisions with rock planets.

The enormous distances in space make the likelihood of an impact within a certain period of time, however it is still advisable to have Jovian planets in order to avoid unpleasant cataclysms.

Alongside this many scientists agree on believing that Jupiter is the source of a number of icy bodies being bombarded on Earth and causing them to change their orbits and, consequently producing large quantities of water to our planet's surface.

The gases in the atmosphere do not just absorb UV radiation, but also in the process, they regulate the complex greenhouse effect.

Venus is regarded by many as being the twin planet of Earth due to its size, mass and location within the boundaries of the zone of habitability. However, as Venus's atmosphere is composed of massive amounts of carbon dioxide, it has a massive greenhouse effect, which generates extremely extreme temperatures even though Venus isn't the nearest star to our Sun!

It may have was awash with water, however solar radiation and greenhouse gases as well as the resulting evaporation of oceans have created the situation the present day as a squally and dangerous planet that is hostile to life.

The greenhouse effect is the fact that certain atmospheric gases which are referred to as greenhouse gases allow for the passage of sun's rays into the layers of the atmosphere and, in the same time keeping the infrared radiation that are emitted by the Earth's surface emitting heat less quickly. This prevents overly thermal imbalances that can cause a genuine homeostasis. It is enough to say that during summer, due to solar rays that are inclined to be perpendicular to the sun, the earth conserves less heat. However, in winter, when oblique rays are reflected that are oblique, more heat is retained.

This balance in the thermostat has been impacted in recent years also due to the rising emissions of greenhouse gases by mankind, which has triggered global debates on global warming.

A few words on the concept of albedo, which is the power of reflection of a material against the incident solar radiation. The greater the reflection the less accumulated heat. A simple idea to keep on the radar, as it is applicable to all objects within the Universe.

We've all heard that darker clothes reflect less than lighter ones, which makes you feel more comfortable. On a larger scale, areas with snow are more reflective than the darker sand or asphalt. These, in reality reflecting less, are more hot than fresh snow.

Europa is an orbiting satellite of Jupiter is covered by an ice dome below where it is believed there are life forms. This ice layer that reflects a lot of sunlight, blocks the proper storage of energy from thermal sources (in combination with larger space between Sun and Europa in relation the Earth).

Determining whether a planet is habitable is not easy It isn't enough to restrict our thinking to things like distance from an orbital star or structure of our atmosphere.

Based on the knowledge of our environment, we could be sure that it is essential to have the magnetosphere. The Earth's central region, rich in metals, produces magnetic fields that stretch thousands of kilometers in space, creating an outer layer known as the magnetosphere.

The shield that surrounds our planet is made up of many lines of forcethat depart from an Pole and then return to the opposite side. While we can't see it with our naked eye, it's enough for us to carry a the simple compass that can be used to detect its existence.

The magnetic field gets perturbed and at the same at the same time, protects (our the atmosphere as well as us living things) against the sun's wind, which is rich with charged particles, and forming an isolated region known as the magnetosphere.

In the vicinity of circular polar rings, you can see spectacular flashes of light caused by the solar wind. In reality the charged particles that interact with the atmosphere release a significant volume of electricity in the form of light. This creates the conditions that allow for the optical phenomenon known as the aurora polaris.

In its existence in the past, the Earth has experienced reversals in its magnetic field.

This would makes it more vulnerable to cosmic rays as well as solar winds. In addition that this could confuse animals like bats, turtles, and birds that rely on the magnetic field only to move and/or movement.

Another factor that could enable the habitability of the planet is existence of a large enough terrestrial satellite (the Moon for us earthlings).

Our satellite initially stabilized the Earth rotation axis. This allowed small oscillations for an extended period of time, and also preventing abrupt climatic shifts (inappropriate to sustain the life cycle).

The Moon is also noted particularly for the phenomenon of tides (the periodic raising and dropping of the ocean's levels) that are derived due to the gravitational pull of the satellite as well as the force of centrifugal due to the planet's rotation in the orbit of Earth and Moon.

The Sun as well as other planets influence our water, but in smaller amounts due to the distances.

In some regions of the world, tides can exceed tens of meters in height, like in the Bay that is Mont Saint-Michel: in these situations, additional variables are at play like water depth along with the shape and size of the bays.

This Moon is also slowing (and is continuing to slow) the rate of the planet's rotation on its axis. It is believed that at first the amount of time needed was one or two hours, which resulted in extremely short periods of darkness and light. Nowadays, things are more complex, with a rotation duration that is much more in line to the notion of habitability.

As previously mentioned that all the elements that allow a planet to be habitable are linked to the one model in existence that is depicted in the Earth.

In the Universe But in the Universe the scenario may be entirely different due to a basic factor: the most common galaxies' stars aren't the yellow dwarfs as the Sun however, but the red dwarfs as well as their orange dwarfs. These two are the subjects of researchers, since they are smaller in mass when compared with the Sun (but still not nearly as big than the Red Dwarfs) however, they're within the main Sequence for a lengthy duration, far longer as our sun, and offer the chance for life to grow and develop.

The orange dwarfs, which are smaller and brighter in comparison to the Sun require an area that is habitable near the Sun, yet not overly to establish the tidal block as well as the synchronous rotation (rotation time that coincides with the duration of the revolution). The planets that are in question may not always have the same features (like the Moon and the Earth) and have the additional benefit of being surrounded by less radiation that is harmful, therefore the protections offered from the magnetic field and atmosphere are but not vital. These hypothetical exoplanetsthat are super-habitable, are better than Earth to be the source of life.

As one of the planets that are candidates scientists are looking at Kepler-442b: the exoplanet, which orbits an orange dwarf within the constellation Lyra is estimated to have an value of 0.836 which is higher than Earth (0.829).

Another issue that is a bit more debatable is the practicality of natural satellites like Titan or Enceladus orbiting Saturn or Europa within Jupiter.

A majority of the satellites within the Solar System do not have an atmosphere, which reduces the chance of encountering extremely simple types of life. Hopes are held below ice sheets, and the proximity of their planets and gravitational interactions with their planets may generate enough heat to permit for the formation of vast oceans made of water.

A bold idea, however not possible, is sending a probe into Europa capable of piercing the ice layer that surrounds the surface (cryobot laser) and drop into the tunnel to create an underwater capsule that is able to explore the deep. This idea is just a theoretical idea, and has to be confronted with the obvious challenges in its realization as well as the delicate process of sterilization that will protect the natural satellite from being infected by microorganisms that live on the earth.

Habitability of the planet is not dependent on the traits that are inherent within the planet. Indeed, scientists are of the opinion that in near future (not too far away) the environment of a planet could be altered to make it habitable.

This kind of idea that is known as of Terraforming comes from an idea that by manipulating the chemicals in atmospheric gas can be altered, thereby ensuring that they are similar to the ones on Earth.

It is an abstract concept, as we don't have enough materials and technology to create an undertaking that is expensive and time.

In addition, creating a healthy atmosphere by Terraforming will not make the planet completely habitable. As an example, we'd encounter the force of gravity in a different way (like in the Moon) and have issues related to medical issues, or in the prevention of the atmosphere from spreading out into the space. The grains that is the magnetic field will be as it is, or be of the right distance to the star.

Venus could provide us with less anxiety due to certain similarities to Earth as well as among the creative ideas of Terraforming, two will be highlighted using solar shields and hydrogen bombardment.

The first option is using huge screens that are placed in space to reduce and disperse sun's rayons. This way the temperatures on the planet will decrease and make the planet more suitable to human life.

The second one is distinguished by the presence of unusual levels of hydrogen that when combined with carbon dioxide will result in water. Because of the planet's cooling water vapor will not just be present when it is gaseous (which will increase temperature because of climate change) however, it could also occur in different state (liquid as well as solid).

The idea of Terraforming is in line with the goals that genetic engineering can bring. One side of the strategy is to adapt an environment to our needs while on the other hand, biotechnology could enable us to adapt by manipulating genes more easily for the remaining harsh circumstances of a particular globe. These are fascinating theories however, they are pure science fiction at the beginning of the 21st century. The continuous advancement of our civilization could eventually make them more than just a few theories.

Chapter 6: The Beginning Of Life

"We are star-stuff, thinking about our celestial bodies." (Carl Sagan[Carl Sagan]

I would like to start this chapter by quoting of Carl Sagan, an astrophysicist famous for his research on Venus, Europa, Titan and the concept of the Voyager Golden Record which is which is a disk that contains audio and images of Earth that travels within both Voyager probes until the outermost reaches of the Solar System, in the hopes that an alien form will be able to locate and understand the disc.

The origins of life is a subject which has been a hot topic of debate throughout the ages. In a way, excluding questions of a philosophical or religious nature, which are outside our scope in this article from an academic perspective living organisms are composed of the fundamental elements namely Proteins, carbohydrates, lipids as well as nucleic acid.

How are these elements created? This is an extremely pertinent question, and the solution to which has been the subject of some extremely bizarre theories discussed.

Before we get into the history of the beginning of life (unfortunately what transpired on Earth is currently the only model we have to study outside of within the Solar System), it is important to emphasize that the existence of planets that are habitable that satisfy all of the above requirements are not sufficient to create primordial life forms, it just increases the likelihood.

The Universe is built on a variety of comprehendable laws, however it is precisely the chaotic nature with its unique nature that make it completely predicable. That's why the concept of the topic of probability is discussed at the final.

The Panspermia hypothesis claims that macromolecules are already present (if they are not monocelled creatures) in space. Furthermore, it is precisely macromolecules like these that fall on planets, thereby providing the necessary conditions for the development of complex organisms.

Panspermia is an objective theory that is neither on its feet or upon the earth. Even if we assume that proteins and carbohydrates exist in the Universe How can they remain unaltered in the heat and stresses of space?

The importance in the role of magnetic fields, or Ozone as a shield against the direct damage caused by cosmic rays and stellar wind has been previously discussed What is the best way to ensure that this protection be achieved for the Universe?

If these microorganisms actually existed what would they do against the force of meteorite or comet (which is their vehicle) with an earth?

The Miller-Urey research is one of the keystones to understanding the origins of life. These two researchers, based on Oparin's assumptions who believed in that life's origins stemmed from the simplest molecules, recreated the Earth's initial atmosphere, which was believed to be composed of ammonia, hydrogen, water methane and other elements, along with electrodes that mimicked lightning and sunlight.

The results were surprising After a couple of days, organic compounds were identified that included amino acids like the amino acids alanine, aspartate and glutamate and glycine. We know that proteins, as important as enzymes, hormones and much more are composed of amino acids.

Miller and Urey might not have recreated the initial conditions in a perfect manner however it was sufficient to make the process of forming organic compounds from precursors of inorganic substances more than just a concept.

As per other researchers, earliest complex molecules would have been formed in the absence of Earth and not in the ocean floor, close to the outlet of volcanoes that were once active The temperatures and energy released would trigger the initial reactions.

The question we should be asking ourselves is what is the source of the primordial soup, either at the surface or under the water that formed the environment for the first fundamental molecules What was the process that led to the creation of cells?

Oparin believed that the lipid molecules formed the form of spheres (the coacervates) and when immersed within water formed the wall (the cell membrane) which was the basis for the precursors to the oldest cells, protobionts.

In the end the macromolecules (such as lipids or proteins) were made from many small molecules. They then aggregated to form more complicated compounds (e.g. within clay) and were held together through chemical bonds.

The issue is that coacervates aren't able to reproduce, and therefore produce an offspring that is more or less alike (and consequently determine the natural selection).

Each theory or experiment has its flaws In Miller-Urey's case, there is the argument that there is an atmosphere that isn't enough reducing and is low in hydrogen too.

On protobionts, there are doubts about the possibility of reproduction and division.

The RNA appears to be the best middle ground because it is both the transmission of genetic codes and an appropriate catalyst to chemical reaction. Protein synthesis, even within the prokaryotic cells (without nucleus) requires RNA which makes it difficult to conclude that proteins formed prior to the formation of RNA.

Life on Earth was born approximately four billion years ago. This was which is half a billion years after the beginning to the Earth itself. actually, stromatolites, sediments made of calcareous material by cyanobacteria, were discovered in Greenland in the early days of.

A discovery made on Venus in September of 2020 of the gas phosphine an unpleasant, colorless gas, has suggested the existence of life on Earth's second planet. Phosphine is made in industrial settings or by microorganisms that are anaerobic, and this discovery can lead us to conclude that there is life on Venus despite the extreme temperatures. Evidently, more evidence is required to disprove or prove this theory. This is why the Earth is unique. the Earth.

Contact with extraterrestrial civilization

Let's suppose it is the case that some time some time in the (hopefully not too far) future , an group of human beings sets out to find the nearest exoplanet Earth. This object, known as Proxima Centauri b, is located in the vicinity of the red dwarf that bears similar name Proxima Centauri.

How was it discovered?

With the advancement of technological advances, planets beyond our solar system are now able to be detected by either indirect or direct detection: We can try to comprehend the planets more clearly.

The principle behind this method is easy: by using ever-growing robust and accurate telescopes, an effort is made to observe directly the planet at issue and orbit around an astronomical star. However the number of planets that can be observed is minimal due to the huge distances involved or due to the light that is emitted by the star's parent (for this issue dimming coronagraphs with stars is being employed with increasing effectiveness recently).

In indirect detection, we do not see the earth however we can recognize it using strategies. The most commonly used is the transit method, and the method of radial velocity.

This method of transit is founded on right assumption of the fact that once a planet passes against its star, it is either completely or partially obscured. Researchers observe this decrease in brightness, and realize that there is a planet orbiting the star. The occultation obviously depends upon the dimensions of the star, the planet as well as the orbit and the alignment to our vision system.

When it comes to the velocity of radial motion is concerned, the logic differs: it's true that planets have an axis of rotation around their stars, but we do not realize that the stars are impacted by the gravitational pull of planets and motion, revolve around a hypothetical central point that is known as the centre of mass in the system.

In the course of the journey it will be observed that the star moves closer to and farther far away, meaning that due to the Doppler Effect we will see an shift to blue (the emission wavelength diminishes) and red (the emitting wavelength rises) and vice versa. Through studying the variations in wavelength in time, we can not only prove the existence of the planet, but are also able to speculate (always within certain limitations) that the environment of an exoplanet.

A good illustration of a shift to blue can be seen in the Andromeda galaxy, which is nearing the one we have (the Milky Way).

One example of a change towards more reds is in the Universe itself that, while expanding, exhibits a progressive retreat of the galaxies that are in the outer regions.

In addition to the features that the stars possess as well as Proxima Centauri b, which is thought to be habitable Our astronauts will have to travel for approximately 4 light years. an astronomical distance that we are unable to cross.

In other words, assuming that the spacecraft could be able to reach the planet within a short period of time What happens in the event that only bacteria were detected within Proxima Centauri b?

On other hand, one will surely be an awe-inspiring reaction to the fact that life exists beyond Earth On the other hand, astronauts will feel a bit of sadness at having traveled for so long and being separated of their family and friends, but not being able to identify intelligent living things.

But how can we define an intelligent being? There isn't a single definition that all people can agree on. ....

It can be summarized as the capacity to confront and resolve new challenges (problem solving) being aware of the surroundings and to remember events, to communicate opinions verbally be able to comprehend an event and to feel emotional.

Animals, unlike humans are more dependent on instinct and instinct, which from one perspective can be considered to be their weak point, since they are compelled to behave in a particular way. humans are, however utilize their imagination to surpass their limits and are not confined by their limitations.

However, studies have demonstrated that animals can be intelligent in different ways (octopuses who are able to open containers or jars as well as crows using branches to capture food and utilize sponges to protect themselves and the arousal of chimpanzees) and therefore demonstrate its existence in the animal kingdom, it is known that human beings are able to show higher levels of development in areas which are responsible for higher cortical function (so-called sophisticated functions).

This is exactly what makes us different and allowed us to be the most powerful on earth. We would like to see on other planets.

The human race over the course of time has not always been the same man is now and has gone through several changes, as small changes which have enabled man to reach the present.

Natural selection does not stare at any creature in the face and is limited to the existence of living organisms that, via the transmission of traits that are advantageous provide advantages in evolutionary evolution.

Jean Baptiste Lamarck, a French botanist and Zoologist from France, was the first to propose that animals were not immortal over the millennia and thus, could develop new characters. His idea was later discredited due to the idea that living creatures were constantly adapting and passing the traits they acquired to their children.

Charles Darwin gave the evolutionary model a push by proposing a notion that generated a lot of controversy in the 19th century's early years. It was believed by the Briton believe that it wasn't animals that needed to adjust to the changing environment, but that the alteration of certain traits that could be passed down and passed on, would result in a better (passive) adaption to the environment surrounding them. Thus, the small traits that were inherited improved the chances to survive and reproduce.

The neck of a giraffe is a iconic example included in Darwin's theory of evolution. It's not as if the cute animals tried to extend their necks to climb higher branches; instead, those giraffes who had developed a random lengthening of their neck vertebrae ate more readily than those with shorter necks.

Natural selection favoured those that had a fortunate evolution, would have less struggle and hence guarantee the survival of the animal species. Just like in the Primates. Also in human.

Homo Habilis was among the first species to employ basic tools for hunting and provided Homo Habilis with a useful tool against larger animals than him.

Homo Erectus utilized this method and, though it is a controversial point it is believed Homo Erectus was the one who first discovered and utilized fire. This allowed one to cook and warm oneself and also to ward off terrifying creatures.

From Homo Neanderthalensis, we can already see the social fabricthat includes the rituals of religious and funerary, and artifacts.

Humanity today (Homo Sapiens) has awoken and understood the importance of agriculture, domestication of animals, which has significantly increased social and cultural organization that has continued to evolve to the present.

When analyzing the diverse human species and gorillas, there is one element that has risen dramatically in brain size. The brain's volume is huge in Homo Sapiens it is about 1300 cm3. In Homo Habilis it is about 600 cm3 and in gorilla, 400 cm3. This is the exact thing that is the reason for Homo Sapiens the ability to adapt to the current day and shape everything that is around us.

If we were to examine the various brain volume with that of Hominidae family. What if we were to consider an animal? Perhaps an elephant?

In this case one must compare the brain's size to the body mass in order to determine if by proportion the man is most prominent.

In discussing the existence of an extraterrestrial civilisation it is important to first consider what the word "civilisation" refers to. In the end, we all return to the human race.

The first civilisations emerged in the last 2,000 years before the time of Christ (B.C.) with the goal to share ideas, beliefs, and traditions ancient religious and legislative aspects, as well as scriptures. The idea of classical writing divides Prehistory in Human History.

In spite of all this we are not satisfiedwith the fact that life is developing on a habitable planet with intelligent life forms, and civilisation isn't enough for us.

The reason? To allow extraterrestrials of this kind to someday contact us, we need technology. Also, it is very advanced.

Emblematic is the first scene in the movie 2001: A Space Odyssey Emblematic is the scene in which Hominids located in the near vicinity of a monolith discover that animal bones can be used to defend their territory from other animals and also to hunt, and consequently consume food.

Through the course of history, a sequence of discoveries occurred one after other, which in turn helped make life more comfortable for human beings however, yet they brought about things that were unimaginable to everyone who lived through the previous centuries.

The wheel allowed to move or move heavy objects using the help of domestic animals.

The idea behind the lever meant that material could be lifted with an inverse force. the idea was later expanded to include objects like scissors.

There are many significant occasions, including discovering penicillin as well as the steam engine, the printing press, the telegraph as well as the development of aircrafts and computers.

However, an alien civilization with the same level of technology as we do is unlikely to ever communicate with us.

From the perspective of reception radio telescopes are able to detect signals coming from an infinite area of the Universe and limit our "hunting" zone. This is assuming one is able to discern these signals.

In terms of exploration How far have we been? We have seen Voyager 1 and 2 probes and the sole evidence of our existence within interstellar space, have only made it to interstellar and didn't enter any other planetary system. Therefore, in the event of this knowledge all of us would be within their own planet with their heads up and hoping something might occur.

It is possible that something could happen if it was due to technological advances, aliens had beyond our understanding and could be able to afford interstellar travel by extending the limits that light travels at (and consequently Einstein's relativity) or using hypothetical shortcuts like wormholes. Only then could there be the possibility of making contact.

Furthermore, there is an additional condition that is often ignored when considering the likelihood for intelligent species and one that Drake has considered in his equation to determine the time span of such an intelligent civilisation.

Let's take a look at some of the greatest empires in history.

Rome was established around 753 B.C., and had the highest level of power under the the emperor Trajan which extended across the Iberian peninsula all the way to Mesopotamia being a king of the time it was completely unimaginable that an empire of this size could be destroyed. However, it did due to a myriad of economic, political and social causes.

Over time, many civilisations have merged, united through expansion, foundation and decline.

Going to a higher stage and focusing our attention no longer to one person instead, but to a whole superorder like the dinosaurs. Their dominance led to their extinction.

There is no doubt about the manner in which it happened, whether through volcanic eruptions, asteroid impacts and sudden changes in the climate, but the fact is their presence was also gone.

When we consider this all at the level of planets it is clear that the two civilizations (ours and the one from another planet) should have a certain time horizon within which they could interact at the same time is striking.

If extraterrestrial civilization had gone extinct long before we could get signals sent from the space area, then no communication with outside would have been possible.

It would be the same situation if human species that went extinct prior to aliens. We hope that this doesn't occur in the near future. It could happen at the earliest possible time.

"Where are all the people?"

With no evidence of extraterrestrial life forms humans are continuously questioned by a deep question: are we the only one in the Universe or do other creatures exist who can imitate our designs (or achieve even greater results)?

There isn't a solution to this problem since our knowledge is restricted to cover a large part of the area.

This "lack" of ours has led to two theories that are in complete contradiction The Rare Earth Hypothesis, and the Mediocrity Principle.

The Rare Earth Hypothesis actually regards the Universe as an environment that is hostile to the growth in complex living. Two Americans Peter Ward and Donald Brownlee declared in the beginning of 2000 the existence of extraterrestrial species were uncommon, but were extremely rare.

The conditions we've already described to be able to identify intelligent living beings that are capable of communicating with us are many factors that need to be incorporated perfectly together and the absence of any one could be detrimental to the possibility of obtaining the life you've always wanted.

The habitable zone as well as the atmosphere of the planet, plate tectonics, and the stability of stars are all vital and the necessity for these elements dramatically reduces the chance of them occurring beyond Earth.

Ward and Brownlee's equation was similar to Drake's and added other multipliers like the proportion of planets with rocky surfaces as well as the outer Jovian planets, and a large sufficient natural satellite and the amount of extinctions occurring on the planet in question.

In increasing the amount of events that occur that are involved in this equation, and thus reaching the sum of these equations, the total number of planets that support complicated life forms is infinitely small.

To this, should be added the gruesome proof that our Universe is comprised of galaxies from different types, and that every galaxy is home to distinct planetary systems, with stars with varying sizes in brightness, stability and stability. A suitable planet must be situated far enough away from black hole and supernova beams.

In a way both Americans are the designers of a skewed cosmic model where man is the sole combination that is currently realized by a variety of dice...

In the end The Rare Earth Hypothesis cynically and brutally solves Fermi's paradox the disappointing solution would be"There aren't any..'

The Mediocrity Principle, on the contrary is a diametrically opposing idea. It can be defined as an extreme variant of the Copernican principle that had completely rewritten the Ptolemaic idea and placed the

Earth not in the middle within The Solar System, but marginally.

The Mediocrity Principle extends even further, removing the exclusive position of mankind and Earth not just in their respective systems of planets as well as in the galaxy and Universe The thing that appears to be unique about us is in fact reproducible beyond our boundaries.

What can we do to prove this hypothesis with Astronomers like Drake as well as Sagan among its staunchest supporters (and simultaneously to disprove it as well)? Rare Earth Hypothesis)?

In the first place, there is the numerical evidence that can be understood by using as a source an image taken from Hubble Space Telescope. Hubble Space Telescope, with the abbreviation HUDF (Hubble Ultra Deep Field) that has been gathering data for more than one year from a small part of the constellation Furnace This image was a collection of many thousands and thousands galaxies within.

Expanding that composition over the entirety of the Universe One study suggests that there are 2 trillion galaxies that surround us (considering limits of our current telescopes). In each galaxy, there isn't only one star (and their planets) as well as a variable number that is made up of numerous figures, the theoretical number is just unimaginable.

In the end, the overwhelming amount of planets and stars will help be able to counterbalance that Drake equation (or the equation from Ward Brownlee and Brownlee) which would guarantee an optimistic outcome, even although not necessarily on the Milky Way, at least within the Universe.

Similar to super habitable exoplanets that orbit orange dwarfs, even though in a very small proportion compared to other planets with rocky surfaces, are likely to be large enough that they could possibly support living to a greater extent because of an estimated habitability index comparable to, or perhaps greater than Earth (Kepler 442 B is mentioned once more).

Another strong argument upon the which the Mediocrity Principle is based on is the nature of the Universe everywhere we look there are inorganic molecules. Imagine the universe as a vast vegetable garden, in the event that the seeds that gave birth to seeds (life in the world of Earth) it is possible to similarly discover others at different locations in the same gardening area (the Universe), given the same conditions for life (habitable zones, atmospheric conditions and so on.).

What happens if the Mediocrity Principle isn't a lie? What is the best way to justify the absence existence of life-forms from other planets? Fermi's query always repeats: "Where is everybody?"

There are many answers to this question. A few of them, which are more than not accepted in the science community will be will be discussed in the following sections.

1.) The first option which is the most simple and understandable is the distance that separates two cultures. To fully comprehend the concept, let's examine instances in order to see the size increase.

Roman legionaries, which were capable of be on the move for extended periods and covered approximately 30km daily. If an army were to move between Gaul (France) across France to Anatolia (Turkey) It would take 3 months or less, covering at most 3000 km.

The Earth Earth has an estimated diameter of 12,700 kilometers, and the measurements already appear to be quite large to us.

The Moon is our sole natural satellite, that seems huge to us from the night sky is 384,000 kilometers away.

And what about the Sun? It is averaging point between the perihelion (minimum distance) and the aphelion (maximum distance) 150,000,000 km from the Sun.

Pluto is an icy dwarf planet that has an extremely eccentric orbit is approximately 6 billion kilometers away.

These measurementsare unfortunately only applicable to our planetary system, which is our Solar System. Should we consider going further?

The nearest exoplanet to Earth can be found in Proxima Centauri B, which is four milliseconds away (making the conversion to 37 trillion kilometers).

What if our highly-coveted civilisation had been on another planet system, like Trappist-1 e? The number of kilometres would rise again (330,000 billion km or 39 light-years).

Let's try to leave our galaxy that is, the Milky Way, and turn towards Andromeda in the limit of 250,000 miles (the calculation of kilometres begins getting a bit more complicated).

Finished? No! Numerous galaxies, some even thousands of trillions of light years away have been found ....

It is evident that spatial distances in comparison to the distances that are typically crossed by the Earth are significantly greater. It is possible that we could be the only one in the Universe However, we're certainly isolating ourselves from each other.

In addition to the notion of distance, we must also consider the concept with time (and speed) since we are all thinking about these two dimensions.

To travel the same route on a plane takes us about 3 hours in the present (as opposed to the 3 months back in 2000).

Two probes, Voyager 1 and Voyager 2 which are that are in space interstellar have speeds of around 15-17 km/sec. Although the speed is much higher than the speeds that are normally achievable on Earth however, it is pathetic compared to the velocity of light which stands at below 300,000 km/sec. If the probes were focused on Proxima Centauri the spacecraft would take 70,000 years to get there, as opposed to just four months for the speed of light.

That's exactly what I had hoped to be, which is that speed at which light travels described as speed that electromagnetic waves travel in the vacuum.

Einstein's famous equation clarifies why it's not possible to surpass the limit, or even get within.

This formula connects energy(E) in relation to mass(m) within a human body beginning with an unchanging c, which is the exact velocity of light. As we speed up (we speak of massive numbers, not something we see every day) it is when a portion of the energy gets transformed into mass, and the result grows. To accelerate more and more, we need to create an ever-increasing amount of energy that will eventually transform into mass. The point will be reached where we'll need an infinite amount of energies to propel a large body. In reality, the more we move the more complex it gets.

We can speculate that Einstein made a mistake in his calculations however, in his favor there are numerous studies conducted with particle accelerators in which no matter the effort you put into it you are unable to break through or even surpass the wall.

The only natural particles capable of traveling in the light speed are photons. They are electromagnetic energy particles that are not mass-based, and cannot be reduced to below this threshold.

Our main limitation lies in the light speed itself beyond which astronauts will never be able to go.

Since they can't traverse the line of sight (as has been the case when sound waves travelled through the air) the time required for reaching the exoplanets of different planetary systems is extremely longdue to the distances described above.

To grasp the enormity of the Universe We could imagine comparing the size of our Earth as a large marble and the rest of the universe to the biggest beach in Brazil What do you compare the marble to those tens of kilometers of sand? A tiny percentage. To travel across an endlessly vast space (the Universe), you require a correspondingly high speed. Unfortunately, we don't have.

From a particular point of from a certain perspective, our space explorations are similar to the very first attempts by Europeans to discover the Americas beginning at the close 1500s (setting aside that Vikings have been the very first people to step foot in the area) as well as James Cook and the discovery of Australia, Hawaii, and the later discovery of Oceania.

What do we have in store for the next few years?

In the near future, with advanced technology, we could make use of rockets powered through the destruction of antimatter and matter (particles with quantum numbers opposite) or control maniacally nuclear Fusion.

The Bussard Collector (which was used as a reference in Star Trek), proposed by physicist by the same name, Robert Bussard, would absorb hydrogen atoms that are in space and, in a reaction, these could be increased to create an amazing jet.

Another fascinating idea (the Starshot) envisages using an extremely thin probe similar to a sail, that is launched into space using an extremely intense laser beam coming from the Earth The speed (estimated as between two and half the speed of light) could allow it to achieve Proxima Centauri b in just two years.

The third and final purpose is a matter of three major issues that hinder its application. The primary issue is that the probe has to focus on a very distant location in space, and as we know, any small error of the distance from Earth will result in an enormous discrepancy when it comes to reaching the location that was previously determined.

The other, which I believe to be more crucial, concerns the inability to stop the probe's movement while it is near the surface of the planet. We would be in the enigma circumstance of having to wait for many years before reaching the exoplanet and then being able to capture images in just the duration of a few minutes because the probe will continue to be swiftly moving along its path but not be able to slow down or alter its trajectory.

The third issue is that the sail, which is very brimming with nanotechnology due to its extremely thin and operates at high speeds, may be severely damaged and irreparable in the event of a collision tiny particles of stellar dust.

The problem, as mentioned previously is that none the ideas mentioned are feasible with the present technology, therefore we must merely be hopeful that an advanced alien civilization will eventually arrive at us (and not the other way around).

Perfect, therefore we can't surpass light speed: But is it possible to circumvent?

Theoretically, yes.

Einstein's General Relativity is based on the concept that the massive cosmic masses are able to bend space around them, creating the phenomenon of a depression (which is our concept of gravity) which causes the Earth to revolve around the Sun for instance.

To comprehend this idea to understand this thought, let us consider the sheet, which is stretched to both ends. Then, place the ball of heavy weight upon it (but not so heavy as to tear it). This object bends the sheet, creating an inclination. What happens when you throw a marble on the sheet? It will begin moving in a circular motion around the ball, only to eventually come to a stop (due the friction) right next to it.

This illustration provides a basic explanation for what happens when space is curvy. What is the case with time?

For Einstein Space and time were not distinct entities, but were one and the same: In fact, it is appropriate to be talking about the concept of SPACE-TEMPLE CURVATURE.

And even then , he was right: it might seem odd, but the truth is that mass doesn't just form a curve in space, but it also curves time.

With extremely precise Atomic clocks, it has been proved (HAFELE-KEATING Experiment) that on Earth that the speed of time is different at different levels (we speak of tiny fractions of one second) and that closer to an object of an enormous mass, events happen slower.

What do Einstein's Relativity be utilized to access otherworlds that are not accessible? By manipulating the space-time.

Wormhole Wormhole (or Einstein-Rosen Bridge) is a form of cuniculus created by folding a particular region of space back onto itself (like an article of paper folded in half) and then bring two distant points closer (which is this case, in the instance of the paper could be altered to coincide).

The Einstein-Rosen bridge therefore is an imagined tunnel that could enable us to reduce time (and distance) while maintaining the same speed at our disposal (obviously lower than light). For another instance it's like traversing it through the Mont Blanc tunnel without climbing it all the way to descend. As we said previously, a hypothetical idea which, according to some, may also indicate the connection point between white and black holes.

Maybe this is the area that scientists need to work on, attempting to break through the boundaries of the Universe by finding ways to make things even possible within it.

2.) The length of civilisations is a second answer to Fermi's query The last factor in Drake(L) equation. Drake(L) equation holds the most important element in the issue, and it is possible to analyze it from multiple angles.

First, we must better define this term, and limit it to civilizations that can communicate and communication. It is clear that a species that is not equipped with technology that is adequate cannot communicate signalling or even receive them.

What about us? How many years have we had the ability to go on?

In this regard, we are an "young" race only having been in the field for just under one century. To demonstrate this it is worth mentioning that the SETI (Search for Extra-Terrestrial Intelligence) Institute, dedicated to the hunt for intelligent extraterrestrial forms is operating for just 50 years.

Also, each message we transmit takes many thousands of years before reaching the intended target 'in the darkness and without science-based proof that anyone is actually there. One of the first messages, called the Arecibo radio signal was broadcast in 1974 to Hercules, the constellation. Hercules which was 25,000 light years away. If we were fortunate (and very lucky, also) we could receive an answer twice as fast time span, or in 50,000 years!

Civilisations shouldn't just send out signals, but they should also constantly send signals.

As a fisherman will cast his rod multiple times throughout the course of his day, and throughout his life in the same way, we must send out signals every day outside of the Solar System, in the belief that some will be recognized by extraterrestrials.

Let's try to quantify the amount that we have put into our work.

The most significant probes that are sent to date comprise four of them: Pioneer 10 and 11 (with digitally engraved images) as well as Voyager 1 and 2 (with sound and images that are from the planet).

The radio signals that are broadcast every day aren't considered because they are too weak and difficult to interpret even when you consider the background noise.

The radio communications transmitted by SETI with sufficient energy and frequency (referred by METI) have a number lower than twenty.

So, at present it is unclear what has been accomplished (within the limitations of our understanding and resources) to expect an solution.

The idea of sending messages to space has been criticized by a few astrophysicistsbecause it would only expose our presence to other intelligent living things.

We don't know how they will react to the evidence for the existence of human beings.

Certain aliens may have rebellious ideas (like those of the Spanish Conquistadors).

Others, scared of a possible conflict may simply seek refuge to safeguard their species.

Others, who have peace-loving intentions, may instead look to create an agreement that is diplomatic and an exchanging of materials (which is the goal we all want to see).

Also, we are a "young race for the receiving of signals from space. While we're developing ever more powerful radio telescopes as well as working within the infrared spectrum however, we are still limited by the limitations of focusing our studies on a tiny portion of space and finding out how radio waves arrive at us.

Over 40 years after the discovery of the Wow! signal, we do not know whether it was an distant signal or stellar turbulent, or simply the closeness of the comet.

It shouldn't be a surprise to much: if, after centuries, we are unable to interpret the Scriptures from Easter Island, or the hieroglyphics of the ancient peoples that are in every instances the expressions from the exact same race located on the exact same world, there's no reason to expect us to immediately comprehend messages from an alien civilization.

What if the problem is in the way we search for them? What if, instead using radio waves we could see the changes in brightness across space as an attempt to communicating? The suspicion isn't just a matter of fact...

In the end, we're like newborn infants just coming acquainted with the new life style that is interstellar communications.

Sebastian von Hoerner, a German astrophysicist, calculated the average time span of civilisations that could be able to reach the distance of 6,500 years and the distance between civilizations in the Milky Way at 1,000 light years.

If two civilizations are separated by thousands of light years, it's likely that one or both of them will end before a genuine dialogue is established. Human research might be able to discern the possibility of the existence of other people however communication will be unattainable because of the distance that is hard to cross.

The longevity of a civilization (able in communicating) is dependent, in addition on the that are intrinsic and external to the civilisation itself.

Over time the human race has grown exponentially, which requires simultaneously growing amounts of food and raw materials.

The development of technology and the growth of population have always been with the use of the natural environment. activities like intensive livestock farming, as well as the genetic manipulation of food items, serve the primary goal of increasing yield.

According to the forecast in the UN prospectus, by the close in the 20th century,, global population is projected to reach 11 billion, which will require nearly 50% more food than currently required, even considering the socio-economic differences that exist on the planet, which can be seen in the inconceivable amount of waste or contrary malnutrition caused by an insufficient caloric intake.

In terms of oil reserves are concern, we don't know when exactly they will expire: although they are estimated to be over a century, take into consideration that oil extraction may occur at ever deeper depths, thereby achieving the longest life span.

What happens when we can not be able to meet our requirements? We'll need to search for alternative sources, master electrical machines and or evaluate and evaluate the power of water.

Then we could arrive at a point where growing needs for development aren't fulfilled by the quality of the latest materials that are available and thereby limiting the growth rate of an entire civilisation (innovation isn't always associated with growth) and the consequent exploration into extraterrestrial life forms.

This possibility, usually thought of as utopian, could be the same for a civilisation that is alien cutting its wings, in the real sense.

Apart from the devastation on the earth, an additional essential factor to take in consideration is the propensity of humans (and possibly extraterrestrials) to engage in conflict.

The increasing destructive power of war has raised fears that wars could endanger any civilization.

Albert Einstein himself, referring to the self-defeating nature of man and self-defeating nature, said: "Man has invented the nuclear bomb, but no mouse on earth would create the mousetrap."

The amount of Japanese who died in 1945 was in excess of 200,000. This includes the ones who died instantly after the detonation of the two nuclear bombs, as well as those who passed away by dying from radiation exposure.

Unfortunately, today's nuclear weapons have the potential to be destructive (in megatons or megatons) hundreds or thousands of times higher than Little Boy and Fat Man of the Second World War: a war between superpowers that involves an arsenal of of these bombs could seriously threaten the future of the human race.

Remember, as we previously mentioned, L in Drake's equation is the time span of a civilization capable of communication. Thus, wars do not need to end in the destruction of intelligent species. All it takes is a drastically reduced amount of living creatures and the destruction that follows and the inability to use the technology on which we're attached and dependent for us to reach an age in which we are unable to transmit or send space signals.

In the absence of electricity and computers or refrigerators televisions and refrigerators wouldn't function and in the end it would be like the times in our Middle Ages, deprived of the amenities to which we were used due to the advancement.

So, we'd live in the post-apocalypse universe after nuclear war, as seen in films and anime like Mad Max or Ken the warrior.

For extrinsic elements that can influence the length of a civilization We should take into consideration all extra-planetary and planetary natural events.

Asteroids could pose a danger to humanity and, in general, to all living creatures living on Earth.

It is important to note that an asteroid can be defined as any celestial rock object (up to several kilometers in size) but when it travels through the atmosphere and hits an object, it is classified as meteorite. It is therefore the meteorite which collides rather than the asteroid. The impact with the atmosphere creates this celestial object (meteor) to "light up and glow, resulting in the mythological phenomenon known as shooting stars (but what star it isn't).

The Earth has been continuously at the mercy of tiny asteroids, however their tiny size and their disintegration when they enter the Earth's atmosphere mean that we're not conscious of their existence.

Scientists monitor carefully in space those mines that cross the planet's orbit and, due to their size, pose at risk in the case of a collision.

Bevan French was already in 1998, when he published Traces of Catastrophe, highlighted the impacts of meteorite collisions on the Earth particularly through a collection of articles in 1998, he explained the ways that craters of a large diameter can be caused by smaller meteorites.

One of the biggest craters in the world can be found in the Chicxulub crater located in Yucatan, Mexico, which is around 30 kilometers in length and was created approximately than 65 million years ago through the impact of a 10-12km meteorite. The collision produced the energy of hundreds of of gigatons (for comparison, Little Boy and Fat Man were in the range of kilotons), while they were fueled by hydrogen. The Tsar bomb was the most powerful weapon ever to explode, with a power of 50 megatons was many times greater than the two nuclear bombs of 1945, however thousands of times lower powerful than that energy released from the meteorite).

The collision created the K-T border (between Cretaceous and Tertiary) and a layer of Iridium (a metal that is mostly found in meteorites) within the rock layers and, most likely, to the mass extinction of dinosaurs.

The impact crater would be the most difficult of our issues in the case of a collision with meteorites of the order of kilometres. There would be shock waves that radiate across tens of kilometers with tsunamis, earthquakes, and tsunamis huge amounts of ash and dust discharged into our atmosphere which could darken the planet and cause temperatures to drop for years, with severe impacts on the flora, agriculture and fauna.

The threat to the civilisation may not come out of space, but instead from the planet itself.

Through the course of time on Earth there have been at minimum, five massive extinctions (termed the Big Five) have occurred and caused significant changes to the ecosystem and the disappearance of living species, and the subsequent change of other species.

One of the major events we've already discussed is the K-T event took place about 65 million years back however, it wasn't the only incident that our planet was witness to.

Around 700 million years ago around 700 million years ago, the Earth was struck by a huge glacier that covered the oceans and land. This theory of the Snowball is a hypothesis which has numerous supporters because of finding anomalies within the rocks across the globe, including glacial deposits or iron-rich sediments.

This massive ice cap did not just completely cover the surface of the earth however, because of the albedo high (and consequently higher reflectivity of solar radiation) an unnatural circle was formed that stopped the planet from breaking away from the grip of glaciers.

It was volcanic eruptions (and their subsequent eruptions) which broke the deadlock actually, by the release of methane and carbon dioxide the greenhouse effect led to temperatures rising and glaciers to melt and overall a situation that was that was more favorable to living.

The volcanoes themselves, who were allies of ours in our time of Snowball Earth, proved to cause devastating effects for the climate as well as living things in our world.

Particularly, the topic is supervolcanoes, the great calderas like Yellowstone Park. The eruptions of'monsters' in this size could not only wipe out the fauna and plants of a continent as well as release such a large amount of ash into the atmosphere, that they created conditions that allowed for a brief but dramatic drop in temperature and to this must be added the issue of acid rains, rich in sulfuric acid...

While major meteorite collisions such as ice ages, massive volcanism have happened only a handful of instances throughout the history of mankind It is certain that any of these phenomena that are that are beyond the reach of humans or a race from another planet might alter the sensitive balance that is the ecological system. If we, currently are the result of those who have survived prior extinctions, it doesn't necessarily mean that we'll have similar luck when it comes to future extinctions (which is likely to occur in the near future).

Special mention should be made to a phenomenon both fascinating and extremely threatening for any civilization The gamma-ray burst.

The gamma-ray blast is an intense gamma-ray jet that is associated with some of the brightest, most powerful and explosive explosions that occur within the Universe. Caused by supermassive star collapsing or through the accretion of matter onto the surface of a black hole the gamma-ray burst is released in a completely unpredictable and random direction.

Adrian Lewis Melott himself hypothesised that one of the Big Five, the Ordovician mass extinction, which occurred around 450 millennia ago was the result of the eruption of a hypernova and the resulting gamma-ray burst.

The gamma-ray burst has been extensively researched because it may end life on Earth forever. The rupture in the atmosphere, along with the intense radiation could never be an ideal match for living.

For us, it is precisely this previously neglected distance that is able to help us It is believed that distant targets may be destroyed in less than the range of 200 light years (not very long but nothing contrasted with the figures that were poured into earlier).

Additionally that, this gamma-ray explosion is expected to be directed precisely toward to the Solar System and, even more specifically towards our planet. A set of coincidences that cannot be easily realized...

The duration of a civilization can be affected by a variety of aspects (outlined in the previous paragraph), David Grinspoon, an Astrobiologist and assistant professor of Astrophysics and Planetary Sciences at the University of Colorado, has developed a theory which I personally consider to be more than a fact.

in his work Lonely planets: the natural concept of life on other planets in which the

American believes that the parameter L of the Drake equation as an indefinite limit up to a certain level. When any civilization grows to the point of perpetually colonizing planets and/or natural satellites, devastating events, even if they are of a certain size may only impact their economic capabilities and communications and still allow them to transmit signals and receive them.

Grinspoon's argument appears to me to be highly valid because, once they've overcome the barriers of their own planet and have a break of it all civilization could grow like wildfire, enhancing proof of the existence of intelligent lifeforms.

For this, obviously you'll need the information to be able to live in different areas, battling and conquering the challenges of planet habitability to which one has to fight.

The extraterrestrial colonisation of space is the future of humanity It will not only allow us to utilize the resources available in greater quantities, however, the colonies themselves will be bases to explore space further and further from Earth Perhaps eventually reaching a world like ours to live on.

A final thought regarding the parameter L is that it is not necessary to consider the length of one civilisation on the planet.

To fully understand this think about an era civilizations could, after an event that was catastrophic, return with the same advancements in technology and thus appear as a suitable to communicate.

In addition, another intelligent species could be a follower and succeed itself on the planet for the duration of its existence.

This is a far more complicated matter than you think because one would need to calculate the amount duration between end of the old civilization and that of the current one (even that of a totally different species) and the amount of instances of intelligent beings that are capable of communicating.

In assessing the length of the life span at Earth (4 billion years) as well as the sheer number of species with high-tech capabilities (only one currently human) and the reality it is likely that the Sun will continue to exist on the Main Sequence for another 5 billion years or more which means that at most, another intelligent animal will be developed (net of the harm the planet is likely to suffer from catastrophes and consequent changes in the planet's habitability).

3.) In averting the two primary explanations that could solve Fermi's paradox (the time and distance of a civilization) Let us dive deeper into the (theoretical) realm of any alien strategy to block contact.

The Zoo Hypothesis suggests that there exist extraterrestrial lifeforms that are technologically advanced but intentionally do not communicate with Earth.

The motive? It's not to hinder our evolutionary process, as humans would do with animals, giving them the natural resources and areas in which they can reproduce and protect their species.

The theory, first proposed within Icarus of 1973 by John Ball, therefore considers that aliens aren't interested to engage with us by studying us and watching us from a distance (exactly like when we were in the zoo).

Extraterrestrials could enable us to expand our knowledge, develop new technologies however, without ever revealing their presence, and without even being aware of their existence. Earth will be a clean natural, uncontaminated space that could evolve completely free of external influences.

The Zoo Hypothesis is a hypothesis that has through time presented two very shaky versions.

The first one is the idea that man has been (and remains) subject to research which means we can conclude that Earth (and generally the whole Solar System) is nothing other than an enormous research laboratory (as we perform in our everyday lives to study the causes of illness and potential treatments).

Human beings is, statistically speaking, likely to be the subject of both observational research (in which the researcher observes without intervention) and research studies. The role for the individual could be reversed and he'd be able to go to be a researcher, to the role of a guinea-pig.

The other variant is called the Planetarium Hypothesis which is the solution to Fermi's dilemma is that we are in an imaginary Universe.

Aliens have created a fictional real world, an illusion which is completely real and obvious to us.

Stephen Baxter, the originator of this idea is of the opinion it is possible that the Universe appears to be empty to us due to the massive Virtual Reality Generator that requires massive amounts of energy.

In this respect I will briefly discuss what is known as the Scale from Nikolai Kardasev, a Russian scientist who classified civilizations in accordance with their levels of technological advancement.

Kardasev I: the civilization can maximize all the potential energy of its planet (man isn't yet at this stage).

Kardasev II: Civilisation can profit from the power of its own planet (especially its star).

Kardasev III: Civilisations can make use of the energy generated by our own galaxies (and that is why the billions of stars).

To harness this energy, the scientist Freeman John Dyson hypothesised a huge structure that could be surrounded by and absorb radiation of stars and be harnessed later: Dyson Sphere. Dyson Sphere (later utilized in numerous science fiction novels).

So, Baxter's generator will require civilisations at the very minimum Kardasev II or III in order to function, giving us the ability the possibility of experiencing a virtual world like the Matrix (always considering the relevant variations).

Apart from the Zoo Hypothesis, an additional reason is The SETI paradox.

Presently, evidence of the presence of aliens has been attempted using two methods:

transmitting or receiving signals that either require the other to be received or transmitted by a different civilization.

Alexander Zaitsev's SETI paradox rests on the right assumption that the search has no value when no one has the need to send signals: the constant searching for extraterrestrial signals in contrast to the more or less complete rejection of transmitting messages to locations that are likely to be visited by intelligent beings.

If we were to try and compare the things humans have tried to accomplish over the past 100 years, between receiving and sending signals, the results will be extremely biased towards receiving only.

If we extend this concept by including all other aliens we can see the falsehood of SETI.

Zaitsev himself stated that "SETI could only be understood only in the Universe where intelligence is built that realizes the need not just in conducting studies, but communicate signals across other potential locations with the same awareness."

The Great Silence would ultimately be caused by the absence of life, but rather to a stubborn attitude of simply listening and avoiding the release of proof of existence at an absolute minimal level.

Extraterrestrial civilisations could also decide not to reveal themselves before us (as for other race of aliens) due to a very basic reason: to be able to live.

If they were to be discovered by mutual contact, it could not be a guarantee of peaceful discussions; in fact the fear of a conflict that could destroy them or make them slaves will force them to communicate or respond to messages from other parties.

It is well-documented that many different socio-politically or religiously-based human civilisations have fought on the planet Earth and the results are often disastrous for both parties (Persians as well as Greeks; Europeans and indigenous peoples of America and others.) It is quite possible that due to the lack diplomatic efforts, this conflict becomes a bending of one civilization towards the other.

Therefore, the absence of evidence for aliens could likely not result from technological barriers rather, it is due to the rational evolution of the species one is a part of.

Science Fiction writer Liu Cixin embraces and expands on this position in her debated Dark Forest Theory.

In a grand scale projection of the natural phenomena that occur on Earth and in the Universe extraterrestrial civilisations could use all the weapons at their disposal to accomplish the same thing that all living things have ever done from the beginning of time: resist the urge to fall.

In addition, as one grows, one requires ever-growing sources, it's not wise to disclose one's place of residence (and consequently, one's material sources).

The Dark Forest is, in the end, a risky game of hide-and seek in which anyone who loses is more than just losing an opportunity to play: predators as well as prey are a part of this unnatural Great Silence and, whoever has a mistake or mistaken belief is exposed, is at risk of complete destruction.

Stephen Hawking himself, as also expressing concerns about artificial intelligence and use of genes for evil, cautioned against sending or responding signals from space: "The outcome could be similar to the time Columbus came to America and it didn't be so good to those Native Americans."

The reason for the decision not to contact us may be explained by another motive or they don't think we are worthy (by because of our technological apathy or ethically unacceptable behavior) or have arrived at a level of tranquility and joy (a kind of bliss) in their own world in which case they feel no reason to fight with any other living beings.

4.) A different solution to Fermi's dilemma was offered by Alexander Berezin in arXiv, as"First in, Last Out..

By using this term (first in first out, last out) The Russian scientist made the truthful conclusion that the very first civilization to be able to afford interstellar travel would eventually be the one to wipe out the rest, even if it was not for any purpose of war.

Berezin has written: "They would simply not observe us because a demolition crew is destroying an anthill in order to construct an property."

If it was just a matter of living space or raw materials, everything will be destroyed, just similar to what happens in natural deforestation.

As per the Russian just because nobody has preceded us and thus destroyed the rest of us (first in) We would become the future demons of alien worlds, making us the last ones to go extinct (last to go).

5) Additional reasons might be due to our current technology, its limitations, or inadvertent usage of it.

There are a few theories according to which researchers are unable to recognize the signals in an right way. Extraterrestrials may, for instance transmit signals with extremely high or low rate of data or even use non-standard (in our terminology) frequency, which could cause them to be difficult differentiate in the background.

It is believed that the vast majority of life on Earth is located around Sun-like stars within the Main Sequence, so we look for targets with the characteristics mentioned above. But what could happen if messages were transmitted from planets that are not part of within the Main Sequence?

Furthermore, one needs to be aware that funds allocated to SETI is not as large, nor are the capabilities of the latest instruments.

In order to detect alien civilisations via radio signals, Earth observers either need higher-sensitivity instruments or must wait for luck that the radio emissions of aliens are more powerful than ours, that some of the SETI programs is listening to specific frequencies coming from the appropriate areas of space; or that extraterrestrials are intentionally transmitting specific signals to us in our general direction.

Chapter 7: The Fermi Paradox Where Is The Rest Of Our Aliens?

The Universe we can observe is huge with the estimated number of galaxies at 2 trillion with a range of just a few million up to billions.

Based on the one and only evidence of the existence of life within the Universe that we have - following an energy source liquid water is regarded as to be the most vital ingredient in life.

The space around a star in which water is able to exist as an element in a spacecraft is referred to by the term "habitable zone and the planets that are located in this zone are referred to as habitable planets.

There are trillions of star clusters that make up our visible Universe contain trillions of planets with habitable life that revolve around them. This is a sign that there are billions of opportunities to develop life throughout the Universe.

We must think who is where?

While having a discussion with other scientists, Enrico Fermi asked that very identical question.

The absence of evidence of of intelligent life on Earth along with the notion that the Universe is awash with alien civilizations has come to be referred to by The Fermi paradox.

The Local Group Local Group

The Local Group is a collection of galaxies that include our own Milky Way galaxy, and numerous other galaxies as well as dwarf galaxies that are all bound to each other through gravity.

Everything that isn't part of the local group is not accessible to us, regardless of whether we could achieve the speed of light in the near future.

This is due to the fact that everything that isn't part of our own local group is moving away more quickly than light due to the influence of the mysterious dark energy.

Instead of focusing on the search for alien civilisations within the Universe let's reduce it to not even the local population, and instead to that of the Milky Way galaxy.

A few estimates suggest that if advanced civilisations can build spacecraft that can support populations for decades to come, then these civilisations could conquer the entire galaxy in between 2 and 10 millions of years.

Drake's equation

In 1961 , Dr. Frank Drake came up with the Drake equation which is a mathematical formula that attempts to take into account all the variables we believe are relevant in finding the amount of communicative and active extraterrestrial civilisations in the Milky Way galaxy.

Let's take a look at the equation and then go through each component one at a time:

N is the number of civilisations that can be detected which should be present within the Milky Way galaxy.

It can be found by multiplying:

R* represents the total number of stars created each year.

Fp, which is the percentage of stars that have planet systems.

Ne is the number of planets in the solar system that have an environment that is suitable for living.

Fl is the percentage of planets where life actually is.

fi is the percentage of planets with life that have intelligent life.

Fc, which is the percentage of civilizations with an technology that can detect evidence of their existence into space.

L is the duration at which that these civilizations send visible signals into space.

Let's discuss putting some numbers in this equation, and then examine what we're having to do with.

A few claim that based on the smallest estimates, the equation appears to suggest that it's highly unlikely for us to be the sole intelligent civilization in the universe, but the main issue is what we consider to be the lowest estimates.'

There is only one aspect of the world to learn from.

We make assumptions about how likely it is life to evolve and the possibility of intelligent beings to develop and for that intelligent life to produce advanced technology and so on. Everything based on one model.

This is why we should take a look at this theory of the Great Filter theory.

The Great Filter

It is believed that the Great filter theory states an element that lead from the creation of life and the time of colonisation cannot be improbable.

Let's trace four important steps along this evolutionary path and examine them in greater detail:

First step: Biogenesis the first step in the evolution of life

Step 2: Creation of multicellular, complex reproduction life

Step 3. The leap to intelligence and

Fourth step: The Colonisation process of our galaxy.

Abiogenesis

There is no definitive understanding of how inanimate chemistry evolved into biology.

As we know all living things within our universe are connected and trace their roots back only one main source of life.

Does this suggest that life is scarce? So rare that it occurs only once in the entire universe or so uncommon that it's an exclusive moment.

That could explain why we don't have any evidence that aliens are out in the universe.

The development of complex multicellular reproduction life

Life could exist on several planets but for it to be complex, multicellular and reproducive is to mean that a specific set of conditions need to be present or created.

Maybe what's happened on Earth isn't as common as we think.

The leap into intelligence

There are plenty of instances of life on our planet, however we are the only intelligent species that is looking to connect with aliens.

It's extremely impossible that any other world be home to aliens who are as us. So what's the chance that these aliens could develop intelligence and the desire to communicate?

Let us look at the animals on earth , for instance.

Are there any species out there which are likely to achieve intelligence that is similar to ours?

Does intelligence evolve in a convergent way?

Convergent evolution refers to the independent development of similar traits in species in which those features weren't present in their most recent common ancestral.

An example of convergence is the eye , which occurs in all cephalopods (such as octopuses and squids) and vertebrates like us.

The evolution of intelligence is a beneficial characteristic to all living things and, in the 100-200 years' time, can we expect that dolphins and crows will develop an intelligence level that is similar to our human intelligence?

We don't have any idea, but the possibility that they could create the possibility that intelligent beings exist more plausible.

The galaxy is being colonised by a group of stars.

Finally, we will turn our attention to the possibility of colonisation in the galaxy.

All of the other great filters are now gone however this one could be in front of us.

What happens to all intelligent civilizations, that isn't quite a way to develop technology that allows them to travel and colonise space and then set them back or even destroys them completely?

An asteroid collision with earth and causing massive extinction, nuclear war, or an out of control changes in the climate that make the planet in which it is located unlivable.

Civilisations that are different types

Civilisations can be broadly classified in Type 1, Type 2 and Type 3 civilisations, based on the amount of energy a civilisation is able to utilize.

The system of scaling was originally developed by an Russian astrophysicist named Nikolai Kardashev and is referred to in the Kardashev scale.

A civilization of Type I can make use of and store all the energy from its planet of origin.

An Type II civilization can harness the energy of their home planet's star parent. This is the capability to harness the full power from the Sun. The best way to achieve this is to employ the Dyson sphere, a possible device that could encompass the entire sun and transfer its energy to the planets that civilisations have colonized.

A Type III civilization - also known as a galactic civilisation is able to control the entire energy in its host galaxy.

Humans haven't yet achieved Type I civilisation and they're expected to be an Type I civilisation within a hundred years or so.

However, there is a significant gap in between Type I and Type 3 and the filter theory that has been discussed before asks whether there's something in between them that prevents Type 1 civilisations from developing into a galactic civilization.

Other options to solve the Fermi paradox

There are several possible solutions for the Fermi paradox ranging from straightforward to the more imaginative and we'll take a look at some them right now.

Aliens are more attractive in virtual reality

Advanced alien civilizations could have created a virtual reality where they choose to be occupied rather than looking for other living things in the Universe.

We're boring

We're uninteresting to a civilisation of advanced aliens and, while they might be cognizant of us, they might not believe that we are worth their time.

They might view us the same way that we perceive ants, however, they aren't interesting enough to attempt to communicate with.

Conclusions

We came to the end of the book, where we began by examining the Drake equation's parameters and then moving into the motivations behind the absence of contact with extraterrestrial civilizations.

On every page, I have chosen to focus on the scientific and experimental area ofscience, while moving away from my own ideas or hopes.

What if we were truly all on our own? What if there's no anyone else on the world? If that is the case, I believe that there's an obligation for humanity to try to keep alive that unique story of life, which is chaotic and random, and to be heard to the deafening and cold space known as the Universe.

I'm leaving to the reader my brief view, which is an argument, similar to it was in the Fermi paradox.

"Where is everyone?"

"They're likely wondering, too."

www.ingramcontent.com/pod-product-compliance
Lightning Source LLC
Chambersburg PA
CBHW060328030426
42336CB00011B/1248